LINDA SEELY

In the Twinkling of an Eye

A look back from the vantage point of Linda's 60th wedding anniversary as though it were In the Twinkling of an Eye from her childhood in Ashton, Idaho through a long and happy life in West Yellowstone, Montana

Opportunity Knocked in Yellowstone
How a humble farm boy became a builder and advocate of West Yellowstone, Montana.
Now including a 2022 Epilogue, in which he tells of happenings since 2016 and the
things of his soul in the twilight of his life.

Paperback ISBN: 979-8-9872930-2-7

Published by Clyde G Seely

White Shirt Publishing

Table of Contents

NOTE TO READER

I feel honored to write *Linda Seely: In the Twinkling of an Eye.* This is a biography of the little girl pictured on the cover, Linda Fischer, who became my wife of 60 years. You will see that the chapters in her book will be called *twinkles.*

I have previously written in 2016 and re-published in 2022 my autobiography entitled *Opportunity Knocked in Yellowstone.* I referred to the chapters as *pebbles.* In case you have not read that book, there are pebbles that deeply involve Linda. For your convenience, I will include those sections and clearly indicate them as "Pebble" chapters. If you have read *Opportunity Knocked in Yellowstone,* feel free to pass over these pebbles. I will only include pebble chapters where Linda played a huge part, as they are her story as well. They will be shared sequentially along with the twinkle chapters.

It is exciting to note that after I started writing Linda's story, who lost her dad when she was sixteen years old, we came across an old trunk with love letters from her mother and dad that had never been read by anyone else for ninety-one years. It was like opening a time capsule! Throughout this book, the reader will be able to read some of those jewels that have changed our lives.

Not only will I be writing about Linda, but I will include, as a condensed permanent record, the lives of her father, Harry (Bud), her mother, Beulah and her brother, Norman. Norman was the last on earth, in that line, to carry the Fischer name. There are also interesting historical side notes about the way things "used to be" that influenced her life and will be forgotten if not recorded.

While writing this biography, I have gained a great appreciation for the word *remember*. In this book, *remember* is used seventy-seven times and *memories* is included thirty-four times. This concept of remembering sets the theme for Linda's biography. The purpose of this biography is to aid us in remembering Linda and to cause all to remember and honor the ones we love.

To remember others shows the love we have for them. To be remembered by others shows the love they have for us. It is worth noting, the word *remember* is used 572 times in the scriptures and is used in both sacramental prayers. Surely, God wants us to remember.

In addition to remembering, I hope this book may also offer perspective. In life, it is seldom possible to know the end before the beginning. However, in this case, I would recommend you read the last chapter (Twinkle 21) first where an 84-year-old writer relates what it is like from this vantage point of being in the *twilight of life*. Years have passed so quickly. Empathetical experiences, from the depths of despair to the pinnacles of happiness have occurred. By reading this Twinkle first, which ends with a light-hearted positive note, hopefully you will be inspired to cherish each day as a blessing as you travel from birth to your twilight years.

Finally, although this book can be read like a novel from start to finish, I have tried to identify the chapters *Twinkles* and *Pebbles* so you can turn to the ones that interest you the most.

INTRODUCTION

"Twinkle, Twinkle Little Star" is a beloved childhood song. The comma seems to separate the twinkles as though there is perhaps a period of time between each. These twinkles will be used as a metaphor representing different periods of time throughout the book. It seems so many years have gone by, as if in the twinkling of an eye.

As I began writing, the word twinkle took on additional meanings. As you search out that early evening star, it seems to twinkle back at you. It appears to shoot out little rays that almost become playful. I have noticed in particular that in Linda's later years, her eyes almost twinkle as she pulls her, by now grown child, grandchild or other child close to her and looks into their eyes as she acknowledges, compliments and even encourages them. Even I have felt and loved that special playful look.

TWINKLE 1

Genesis of the Name for Linda's Biography

I am only one, but I am one. I cannot do everything,
but I can do something. And I will not let what
I cannot do interfere with what I can do.

—Edward Everett Hale

Linda and I were on our way to Salt Lake City to meet up with our family and friends to celebrate one of those momentous decade birthday parties. We had reserved a private meeting space at The Roof, in the Joseph Smith Building for a wonderful meal and a place where anyone who wanted could say a few nice things about this wonderful lady that I had been married to for 57 years. I was driving, which was our normal routine. We always started with me driving, until my eyelids would get heavy, then we would switch. While Linda drove, I would catch a nap during our six hour drive. Well, this time I had her stop the car but instead of being sleepy, my mind raced and I started writing down on a piece of paper the words that came flooding into my mind about her.

I couldn't believe how fast the time had gone! I had known Linda as the little girl, pictured on the cover of this book. Days turned into years but it seemed like only a moment as they flew by in the twinkling of an eye. At the appropriate time, after the meal and desserts were finished, I read off my marked-up handwritten results from my napless ride to Salt Lake. I titled this little poem as, you might have guessed, "In the Twinkling of an Eye."

"In the Twinkling of an Eye"

To Linda
November 1, 2019

'Twas five in the morning when I picked up my bride,
to the temple we went, and were sealed just inside.
The little girl with the big dark brown braids
Had turned beautiful; My single life I was so willing to trade.
Across the altar she said, "YES", through a
flood of tears in a sacred grip.
And then with a $.25 hamburger we started our trip.
Through this happy reunion our little children numbered five.
One was called home at 29; To live together
again- we will strive.
Farm life was traded for a new adventure at Three Bear
And after 57 years we are still happy to be there.
Through troubled times she was the wind beneath my wings.
Encouragement, love and support to our
marriage she always brings.
To newlyweds, I have often said, about love you
know nothing yet,
True love is built and tested overtime and is still yours to get.
We have been blessed to travel the world over
But our family and home we would trade for no other.
From your mother came your gift of light conversation

In that you take the forefront, while I have a great reservation.
What you could do for others, there is no limit
for such a trait, who would want to trade it?
We have gathered here tonight for a Feast in
honor of a great lady.
Where did all those happy years go? Is it a ruse that you are 80?
Though I may try, it doesn't matter what I can do.
For it only feebly expresses my love for you.

Happily growing old together.
All my love,
Clyde

1 Corinthians 15:52 says, "In a moment, in the twinkling of an eye, at the last trump: for the trumpet shall sound, and the dead shall be raised incorruptible, and we shall be changed."

TWINKLE 2

Linda's Forefathers

Linda was Born in the hospital in St. Anthony, Idaho November 5, 1939, to Harry (Bud) and Beulah Young Fischer. Linda's earliest recollections of family life were when her father worked on a ranch just south of Henrys Lake, Idaho. She, along with her older brother Norman, lived in a small two-roomed cabin in the summer while her dad worked on a cattle ranch. The following winter they would move to St. Anthony, Idaho.

Fishing was great as was proven by Norman. He was three years older than Linda and he liked to go sit by one of the creeks, near a culvert. He would wait there with his hand close to the water. When a big fish was just lollygagging along, swimming just enough to withstand the current, Norman would grab the unwary fish and pull it out of the water. I suppose there was never a shortage of fish to put on the table. Perhaps this is why Linda has never cooked for our family, much less eaten fish in our house, and why most of our kids do not like fish.

Linda's uncles, Cy and Les, would often come up from St. Anthony and fish as well. They were always successful in catching a large mess of fish. Then, little Linda and her cousin Sally, Cy's daughter, would drag the fish in a big net to the car, only to turn back to retrieve more. Except when the fish was too big like this one.

Uncle Cy caught this fish while visiting. It was too big
for Linda and Sally to drag up to the house.

Uncle Les was given too much drink (a little softer way to say alcoholic). Throughout most of his life, he spoke with a loud voice and was quite a colorful character, to say the least.

While I was growing up, I also knew him. He was sometimes intimidating to be around. However, eventually, he righted his ways and became a very successful county commissioner in Fremont County, where he was well respected.

Later in life, he shared with Linda and I this story. One winter, while staying in Island Park, he and his dog got snowed out from his cabin. Even though it was dark with the wind howling and the snow blowing they had to get back to his cabin. Les said he would walk a little, then pull out his bottle for a little warmth and encouragement. Then thinking that if the alcohol made him feel better, it should also make his dog feel better, so when he would stop to take another drink, he would pour a little for his dog. This continued until they finally made it home where both he and his dog crashed for the night.

In the morning, of course Les reached for his bottle and started to walk across the room. The dog, on seeing this, struggled to get up then ran to the door with his tail between his legs, clearly afraid of the contents of that bottle.

In the days of the silver dollar, Les made the statement that was so typical of him, "Them there dollars are made round to roll." And roll them he did.

Les was a real tease. When Linda was little, he would come bursting into the house and say to her, "Where's that old sheepherder dad of yours?" Linda would bristle and say in a disgusted voice, "My dad is not a sheepherder, he's a cowboy."

Linda's other Uncle, and Les's brother, Cy was a sheep man and so were the Seelys. We often ran sheep together. However, Linda's dad was a cowboy. There has always been a feud between the sheep and cattle men. At our wedding reception, when Cy had the mic, he settled the controversy by saying, "Well, these two have accomplished something that very few have, the marriage of the sheep men and the cattle men."

Linda's next memory includes living at the Railroad Ranch, in the southern part of Island Park where her dad and mother worked. She liked living there because there were so many things to do. She loved to ride horses. Much time was spent riding around the ranch.

The first winter that she was old enough to go to school, her dad stayed to work at the ranch while she and the rest of the family moved to Ashton, where she spent the rest of her childhood.

The Railroad Ranch was owned by the Harriman's of railroad fame. This 15,000-acre ranch, just south of Island Park, Idaho was operated as a cattle ranch and Linda's dad, Harry (Bud) helped take care of the large cattle herd in the summer and stayed to feed a few cattle and horses in the winter of 1945.

The name Railroad Ranch may conjure up images as a herd of locomotives gathered in a rural setting. Actually, there was not even a railroad track for many miles until E.H. Harriman built one in 1907-08. In 1905 Harriman rode the Butte Special passenger train which stopped at Monida, Montana. From here, he took a 60-mile stagecoach ride to what would become West Yellowstone. The next year he started building rails to West Yellowstone. Long after Linda lived there, E.H. Harriman's sons, Averill and Roland, who used to come and enjoy this scenic, wildlife area as kids, donated the ranch to the State of Idaho in 1977. It became Harriman State Park, one of the first State Parks in Idaho. It is home to 2/3 of the trumpeter swans that stay in the country for the winter.

Edward Henry, (E.H.) Harriman, their father, was the President of Union Pacific Railroad and had built the museum quality 1903 OSL Vice Presidential car which we eventually owned and now sits in the Holiday Inn in West Yellowstone where it is open to public viewing. Readers of my biography, Opportunity Knocked in Yellowstone, will be able to read much more about the unique history of that railroad car and how it arrived here.

Each of our lives are molded into who we have become by those who we looked up to in our youth. Like Linda's uncles, other relatives have gone on to a state of happiness that hopefully one day we may be with each other again. Her predecessors who have lived exemplary lives have been an influence on our own. Linda and I not only have had a wonderful marriage for 60 years with a mutual love and respect for each other but have found that we are not the first. Our families have been crossing each other's paths for years, long before we knew we would form that eternal bond of marriage.

Credit must be given to the forefathers who came to the Fremont County, Idaho area. In Linda's case, I would like to mention at least two. Linda's great, great grandfather, Israel Justus Clark and her Grandfather Stillman Young.

Israel Justus Clark

Linda's maternal great, great grandfather is Israel Justus Clark. He was born December 25, 1821 in Ossian, Allegany, New York and died Sept. 13, 1905 in Vernal, Utah when he was 84 years old. Israel was just seven years old when his father died leaving a large family. At 13 years of age, he began working as a carpenter learning how to use the lathe and build chairs. He was on his own after that and never saw his family again.

Israel Justus and my great, great grandfather, Justus Azel Seely, though older, undoubtedly knew each other. Israel Justus Clark owned property in Nauvoo, Justus Azel Seely owned property across the Mississippi River in Nashville. Both had a common name, Justus. They both lived there when Joseph Smith was martyred and I'm sure they grieved at his martyrdom.

He joined The Church of Jesus Christ of Latter-Day Saints on March 9, 1844 at the age of 23. He came across the plains to Utah with the John Smith Company, in the Brigham Young group. He was truly a pioneer, an outstanding colonizer, builder and great friend to the Lamanite people. He spent nearly 50 years of his life among the Indians as a missionary. He was an Indian interpreter and could speak their languages perfectly.

In 1859, Israel Justus Clark was one of the original pioneers to Logan, Utah. In 1867, he moved to what is now Clarkston, Utah where he was the first bishop of the local ward. Clarkston was named in his honor. It also is where Martin Harris is buried.

Israel was a very likable man, standing 6ft. tall with auburn colored hair. It turned white early in life, which gave him an almost prophetic look. He had keen blue eyes, if needed they could stare an Indian down, yet twinkled when talking to a child. His voice was clear and loud.

His carpenter trade was put to good use in Ashley Valley, located southeast of what is now Vernal, Utah, which he helped homestead. Much of the coffins in that valley would be made by Israel. He helped to build churches, with schoolhouses and furniture being his specialty. Most likely he developed these carpenter skills from training in his youth. Later in life, he was blind for several years. He died on Sept. 13, 1905, before his 84th birthday, and is buried in the Vernal Memorial Park.

Jenny and Stillman Young

Linda's grandfather on her mother's side was Stillman Young. He was born June 9, 1872, in Princeton, Minnesota, the youngest of 9 siblings. His father died when he was just three. His mother joined

The Church of Jesus Christ of Latter-Day Saints and decided to go to Utah. Part of the family stayed behind while she and the two boys, Stillman, 5 and Charley, 8 moved to Sanpete County, Utah.

The first shoes Stillman had were made by his stepfather. He remembered going out in the snow and seeing the funny tracks he made.

In 1891, he came to the present site of St. Anthony, Idaho where he worked at a sawmill on the Fall River Canal, in Twin Groves, Idaho. In 1892 he met his future wife Elizabeth Jane Clark (Jenny) who was cooking at the sawmill. Stillman and Jenny were married January 1, 1894.

In 1893, Stillman had filed on a homestead of 80 acres in Twin Groves. When they were married, they moved to live on the land. In October of 1895, Stillman and Jenny traveled to Logan to be sealed in the Temple. The trip took 5 days each way. They had one little girl at the time, Faunt Eliza. Six more children were born into this union: Myrtle, Lester, Blanche, Eunice, Cyrus and Beulah, (Linda's mother).

It is intriguing to me that the Seely/Hansen and the Young/Clark family's lives have run parallel since the time they joined the Church in Nauvoo, Illinois in the mid 1840's and traveled across the plains to Utah and then to homestead land a mile from each other in Idaho, much less a little country farm area called Twin Groves, Idaho. I don't know at what point they became acquainted, and their lives became so intertwined.

My Grandfather Soren J. Hansen was called to be the 4th Bishop in the Twin Groves Ward and Linda's grandpa, Stillman Young was his 2nd Counselor. Linda's Grandmother Elizabeth (Jenny) Young was the Relief Society President for 19 years and my grandmother Annie Hansen was her 1st, Councilor.

My mother, Oneta Hansen and Linda's Aunt Faunt were best of friends. Mother told us kids that Fauntie, as she called her, would come over to where they were living. Mother said, "I was fat and she was skinny. One time I was getting ready to go to a party and couldn't get into my dress. I got a pair of corsets with the strings in the back, and we went into the chicken coop to try to get me into the corset. She would tug and pull on the strings and then we would start to laugh.

She would put her knee up on my back side and pull some more. And then we would laugh some more."

I imagine it was a rather funny sight. I wonder how the chickens reacted, if some of those cackles weren't chuckles?

> This reminds me of a time that I related in my book, about Dad calling me in the middle of the night because he thought a skunk was in the chicken coop. In our white underwear but not without Dad remembering to put on his hat, we stealthily approached the chicken coop. The skunk must have seen a couple white figures coming, and the chickens calmed back down to a few clucks.

TWINKLE 3

Linda's Parents

In general, life was simpler in those days. The home and family lived in their own little world, uninfluenced by the array of electronic gadgets. Linda's parents taught the good old-fashioned values of honesty and kindness. Children were expected to "behave yourself," a term we don't hear much anymore. Her dad and mom set a good example for their kids, Linda and Norman.

Linda said this about her parents, "They grew up with a good work ethic. If you take a job, you do it well and be considerate and willing to help other people. They taught me how to be who I am." Linda and her brother Norman learned a lot about life from them.

Her parents looked forward to socializing with friends and would especially like to go to dances at Ponds Lodge in Island Park. Linda said, "They would all bring their kids and put us in a room where we played. Someone would check on us periodically and would bring us popcorn." Dancing must have been a main source of entertainment in those days. Her grandparents on both sides were excellent dancers as they could 'flow across the dance floor.'

"Bud" Fischer

Harry Foster Fischer

Harry "Bud" Foster Fischer, Linda's father, was born April 7, 1910 in Buffalo, Johnson County, Wyoming. Bud passed away Jan. 31, 1956 from a heart attack in Ashton, Fremont County, Idaho.

How do I write about a man I have never met, who was the father of my bride? How could I tell of those missing years that became somewhat mysterious? How could I reach into the past for those who had special memories, when most of them are also gone by now? Up until recently, I could only relate to stories I have heard about this phantom of a man, which is what Linda's dad has always seemed to me.

Linda's mother, Beulah, passed away April 10, 2007. She talked little about any warm and personal stories of Bud which contributed even more to the mystery.

I can write down stories I have heard Linda tell, but she only knew him for a short 16 years of her life.

I will briefly mention here that a newly opened travel trunk of Linda's mother, Beulah, was opened just a few weeks ago and revealed a treasure trove of love letters between Bud and Beulah. These were written in 1932 and 1933 before they were married and then again in 1945 after marriage when Norman and Linda were little. It was when Bud worked at the Railroad Ranch and spent a long lonely winter, that he wrote to his wife and two kids, Norman and Linda.

When Linda was little, she never knew Bud was her dad's nickname until someone came to the door and asked her if Harry was there? She said, "Harry, who?" It was in this trunk where we found out when he received that nickname.

For us, this trunk was like a time capsule. Sealed for 91 years, it at last was opened to us, which became a life-changing experience to handle keepsakes previously not known to us. In those short 16 years of life, Linda only knew one side of her dad, and I never knew him at all, so looking into Linda's parents' old trunk changed all that, as we discovered more private things about their lives.

Before finding the trunk, I had already started writing what I knew about their lives together. I will leave that unchanged. However, the exciting discovery of the keepsakes and contents of the trunk will follow. This is also to tease the reader, hopefully with a fraction of the anticipation for the exciting things that we found there. So, stick with me, as I can assure you there is a *trunk* that will be opened, and you can vicariously peer inside at that time.

Linda's dad, Bud was born in Buffalo Wyoming along with his sister Birdie to Ed and Dell Fischer. Ed was one of the first to make homemade beer in Buffalo. They moved to St. Anthony where

Harry F. (Bud) Fischer eventually met his soul mate and married Beulah Young on November 4, 1933. To this union, Norman was born August 23,1936, and Linda was born November 5, 1939, in St. Anthony, Idaho.

Bud, in later photos, seldom had his picture taken without a cowboy hat. That was just who he was. In later years, when his hat did come off, his forehead was normally lighter than the rest of his sun-tanned face. After working at the Railroad Ranch, Bud did several things to make a living for his family. They lived in Squirrel, Idaho where he leased a farm and then in Ashton where he raised potatoes.

But his passion was working with and being around horses. He became the Idaho State Brand Inspector, which required him to attend livestock auctions at Rexburg and other places. It was his job to make sure when the animal was leaving the State that the brand was transferred to the new owner properly. Linda tells me that Bud would take his dog, Trixie, and throw his coiled-up rope in the pickup and was off for the day. That rope came in handy sometimes when he would see his nieces and nephews and, for fun, would rope them like they were a calf.

He could also do tricks with a rope. He would spin a big circular loop and hop in and out of the loop as it was spinning parallel to the ground, mirroring a skipping rope's rhythm. Then he could spin it out to the side with a big loop and jump in and out of the loop. He would also do a big loop standing inside it and make it go up higher than his head and back down to nearly touch the ground. All of this while he was wearing his Stetson hat.

Bud had his workaday ritual. But his real joy in life was rodeoing with his favorite horse Messa. He would travel around to the local rodeos, often taking his family with him. It seems that every town had a rodeo ground, with wooden shuts and grandstands. St. Anthony and even Twin Groves, where I and Beulah grew up, had them. When Linda was still a little girl, sometimes Bud would have her ride his mare, Messa, around the outside of the rodeo grounds to keep Linda calmed down. Messa was a beautiful dark brown chestnut in color. When it came time for Bud to participate, it seemed as if Messa knew she was about to perform, like the blood and excitement would start coursing through her veins. Linda said she felt that same feeling, when she was waiting for and watching her dad perform.

Bud was a stocky person in his chest and shoulders which helped him become really proficient when the bulldogging event took place. For that event, a steer would be turned out to get a head start. At the same time Messa and Bud would start on the dead run getting next to the steer. Bud would lean way down and to the side of the saddle until he had grabbed the reluctant participant steer's horns. (Can you imagine doing that? The first guy who invented that little stunt must have been bucked off a bull and landed on his head a few to many times.) At just the right time he would leave the horse, and with his heels dragging in the dirt, and his body twisting the head of the steer sideways, he was able to pull the steer off its four feet and down onto its side. Of course, all who participated in the bulldog event were timed, with the fastest being the winner.

Here is a sneak peak of a letter written from Bud to Beulah (found in the trunk which you will learn more about shortly) regarding a bulldogging mishap. Bud had ridden at the 4th of July Rodeo and from a letter to Beulah, dated July 8, 1933, we read:

> *We had a good show, everybody was pleased. I was stiffened up some. I nearly had a couple of ribs broken, when I started to fall on to my steer in the bulldogging. I missed him and tore up about a ton of gravel with my ribs. I won third money in calf roping and got bucked off in professional bronc riding. Serves a fellow right where he gets too reckless.*

Bud was also very good at cow cutting, for which he won a trophy. He also was good at calf roping. At these events, there was great excitement in the air. Linda shared seeing the horse's excitement at these events as it would prance around while waiting for that nudge by Bud to leave the pen. Then in one leap, the horse was off on a dead run after the calf.

With calf roping, the rider must be careful to lean into the start and have a feel of the horse, or he might find himself left behind on the ground. If the calf was given a head start or if the horse broke through the trip rope before the calf got his head start, there was an automatic disqualification. The time started when the trip rope was broken. Then the cowboy, slinging the rope over his head in a circular motion, would throw it around the calf's neck. Then the cowboy would leave the horse, run up the rope and throw the calf to the ground, tying all four feet together so the calf can't get back up. Bud was able to do all this in 11 seconds and won the event.

In those days, it was hard for rodeos to pay adequately, considering all the traveling and time spent in preparation and feeding your passion. But Bud was good enough to win a little cash, trophies, and belt buckles. Linda and I even inherited his prized saddle won at a big rodeo.

Bud was stern when it came to table manners. Linda and Norman were raised to be respectful to their mom and grandparents. Bud also let it be known that he didn't like to have to repeat things he wanted done, like certain chores, etc. Neither Beulah, nor he, were given to show much affection in front of others. Bud never used endearing nicknames like "honey" or "sweetheart" in public. Linda has talked about this family relationship many times to me, not in a negative but respectful way.

Bud was a social drinker and Linda never saw her dad inebriated. He smoked, but not in excess, and Linda does not recall him smoking in the house. His language was respectful to others and swearing was done discreetly. And, certainly not around Beulah's parents.

When Bud was young, his mother joined the Catholic Church. He attended church in St. Anthony on Christmas and special occasions. Beulah, on the other hand, was baptized in The Church of Jesus Christ of Latter-Day Saints when she was eight years old. She attended church occasionally after they were married. But out of respect for each other and not wanting anything to come between them, they decided that religion was not going to be an issue or cause for any discord among the family. So, they would go their separate ways as far as religion was concerned but mostly, they spent Sundays together.

Bud, Beulah holding Trixie, Linda and Norman. This is the last photo we have of the family before the tragedy happened.

Bud was a healthy guy, as you can imagine based on what has already been shared. At the beginning of 1956, in connection with a job he was applying for, Bud needed a physical. Linda remembers him coming home and telling them that Dr. Larson said he was in great shape. However, on that next night, on January 31, the unexpected happened.

Norman was in Utah at college and Linda was upstairs in bed. Her mom came rushing upstairs and told Linda, "Something is not right with your dad." They went back down to the living room and Bud was sitting on the couch. Just as Linda came into the room, he laid his head back on the couch, took a deep breath and was gone. He was just 46 years old; Beulah 44, Norman 19 and Linda was 16 years old. He had lost in his life's last rodeo and now there was a different kind of emotion that followed.

Dr. Larson came and was incredibly kind to them. He asked if he could do a partial autopsy to see if he had missed something. In a follow up letter to Beulah, he shared that from the results he had a massive blood clot lodged in his heart. "This type of heart attack can hit any of us irrespective of any previous heart trouble, so I guess his death was largely a matter of fate." The blood clot was the 'reason' for his early passing but the 'why' was a matter of fate. We can only realize that we are all subject to a Higher Power and that someday, from the vantage point of the future, we will understand.

They lived in the little gray house that has been uninhabited for years and looked very shabby, when I took the picture for this writing in 2022 (pictured later). There was a living room and kitchen on the bottom floor and two bedrooms on the second floor. One for the folks, the other for Norman and Linda to share. When passing this little house on the highway in Ashton, Linda often says. "I wish they would just tear down that house."

Previously, Bud had come home one day with a new 1955 Chevrolet car. It was a complete surprise to the family. He said Hemming, a friend and Chevrolet dealer, had given him a very good deal. This was the first new car they had ever owned. He financed the car and Hemming had talked him into taking out an insurance policy on the car. Beulah was really surprised and of course said, we can't afford it. But Bud assured her it would be okay. To her great surprise a few days after Bud's death, Hemming came over to see the family and handed them the title for the car. Bud had insured it and the car was paid for in full.

The Trunk

Recently, we opened Beulah's trunk that had not been disturbed since she last opened it before her passing. This was a treasure trove of interesting information and insights that Linda never knew about. As could be expected, there was a whole different insight into and appreciation for her dad when she saw the contents of the trunk, as you will see later. For me, it served as a late introduction to the man whose little daughter I married 60 years ago. Reading journals of years gone by pales in comparison to finding physical things that you can see, feel and read, knowing they belonged to your loved ones. I hope this record will serve as a life story that was never written by Bud or Beulah but will now be preserved for future generations.

Keepsakes hidden in Bud and Beulah's Trunk

Ironically, several months after finding and opening the trunk mentioned above, we found a second 'treasure trove of information.' We discovered another tote that we had not looked deeply into before. It had Bud's cowboy boots; the original ones that Norman had painted, the painting of which has always hung in a prominent place in our home. Above that painting, I have now hung those original black boots. The accuracy and detail are amazing.

In that tote, were personal writings of Beulah and Linda. I will mention them now as a precursor to the letters that will later be shared. Also included was a newspaper article about Bud that I will include under his information and Norman's information will be under his name.

Found in the trunk was Beulah's handwritten sketch of her life. (Typed here in 2023 by Clyde)

> I don't think anyone could have a greater heritage than to be born of goodly parents, to have a home where there is love for one another and parents we could always turn to for guidance and advice. This we certainly had. In any large family it takes a lot of work to teach trust, confidence and understanding. There is always anger, hate, and jealousy to be controlled. Speaking of controlling tempers, I always thank my mother for making me control mine. I had a bad temper. I would come home from school or play so mad and mother would always say – now when you get that temper under control we will talk about it and not before. I spent a lot of time sitting on the chair! But I've thanked her many times for having the wisdom to do this.

> I often think back to the time I was married and the advice my dad gave me. I told him I wanted to marry Bud. If that is what you want, fine. He is not a member of the church but a good fellow. Remember one thing though – do not let religion wreck your marriage. I did remember that advice always. And my marriage was a happy one.

> I have many wonderful memories of my own life and the teachings of my parents.

> One thing that happened just before Norman was born; I remember very clearly. I came to mothers one day and I was really mad. I was not controlling my

temper. I said, I'm so mad at Bud Fischer, I just think I'll get a divorce. My mother's answer was – well just remember Beulah you are a lot harder to live with than Bud is. That statement came to my mind quite a few times after that.

Anyway, if I can leave a few good memories with my family that will be what I want to do the most.

Linda's high school report, written January 18, 1956, begins with: *Dedicated to my Father and Mother.*

As fate would have it, her father died January 31, 1956, just 13 days after she submitted this report. She concludes her report on a separate page with the following:

My Future

I hope that I can make something of myself in the future. It is my hope to go to college and then work for a little while. It is also my hope to get married in the L.D.S. temple and raise a family. I would like to thank my parents for everything I have done and everything I will do in the future.

Even though she was not a member of the church at the time, because of the wish of her dad to wait, she was eventually baptized and, in my estimation, has fulfilled her own goals of the future very well. I'm glad I was included. Some of the interior of the report will be included elsewhere.

In Beulah's trunk, as you would expect, were lots of old photos, high school yearbooks, graduation and school documents, sympathy cards, Catholic study manuals, Bud's rosaries, accounting/ bookkeeping manuals, old newspapers, Bud's trophies for various rodeo events, sympathy cards to Beulah and kids when Bud died so suddenly. Also, his old wallets, well-worn from sitting in the saddle so much, were there.

But most exciting and almost life-altering were the letters dated 1932, 1933 and 1945 from the following times in their lives:

1. There were love letters to Beulah from Bud, complete with 3 cent stamps.

2. There were letters, (eventually love letters,) from Beulah to Bud.

3. Love letters from Bud to *Dearest Beulah and kids*. (It was fun and easy to read between the lines to know what they were talking about).

4. There were 95 sympathy letters, after Bud's death, to Beulah and kids.

Reading these letters was like looking into the souls of those we knew relatively so little about. What was in those *love letters*? We were almost giddy with excitement as we started going through them. Of course, the thing we wanted to know first, was how they felt about each other and what they talked about while dating and after marriage. As mentioned earlier, Linda never heard her parents use any words that expressed affection. So, we were excited to read, if they started with more than just, "Dear" and ended with more than just, "as ever."

Well, we were elated by Bud's letters and Beulah's letters. They said words that showed a softer side of her parents, words Linda never dreamed her parents would have used. But there they were.

I will start by referring to Bud's letters to Beulah in 1932.

They mostly began with "Dearest Beulah" or "My darling Beulah." You can see how they got closer over the two summers they were writing. I will relay a few of his closings.

> *I have been thinking of you all day and am wondering if you think of me once in a while.*

> *Lots of love, if you will allow me to say it.*

Another, *Lots of love and a Kiss. Hope to have a couple arms full of love soon, As Ever, Bud.*

He also had a sense of humor.

Will close for now and go to bed thinking, thinking, thinking, thinking—how sleepy I am. Lots of love.

What I thought was a rather stoic relationship, has turned into a love story that only enhances our feelings for them.

The Mind Cannot Forget What the Heart Loves

I love the way Bud closed three of his letters. I do not know if he originated this, but I suspect he must have told this to Beulah when they had seen each other and then followed up in letters. It has become a favorite quote of mine

At the bottom of three letters, Bud ended by saying,

And remember, my mind doesn't forget what my heart loves.

June 5, 1932, he ended with:

Guess that I better say goodnight, sweetheart, for this time, for me. Remember what I have told you and I think of you quite often for, "The mind cannot forget, what the heart loves!"

On July 11, 1932, he closed by saying: *Remember, I cannot forget the one my heart loves.*

I would like to couple this with one of my own observations that has become apparent as I have been writing this book which is, "Remembering causes us to preserve the memory." Put those together and it becomes a never-ending circle of love. That is what we are doing, by remembering their past it causes us to preserve their memory for generations to come. Hence, the purpose for writing this biography.

It was fun to read what turned out to be a theme running through his letters. He continually wanted Beulah to write. After all, he was out on a cattle ranch in Lakeview, Montana, sometimes cold and lonely.

In order to understand and more fully appreciate Lakeview, I think it will be interesting to tell you where it is and of the significance of this little known, or appreciated area. Lakeview, Montana has a population of fifteen and is situated about halfway between West Yellowstone and Monida, Montana. But if you want to go on current designated roads, it is like, "You can't get there from here." Even though it is only 30 miles, half of it is on an old stagecoach route.

The beginning of West Yellowstone, Montana was considered to be 1908, when the railroad arrived. Before the trains arrived, people would come on the Butte Special, from Salt Lake City, and get off at Monida, Montana. There they would take a 60-mile stagecoach ride past Lakeview, to what is now known as West Yellowstone. They would then take stagecoach tours of Yellowstone. Such was the case with E.H. Harriman, President of the Union Pacific Railroad. He passed through Lakeview on the stagecoach, and after seeing the wonders of Yellowstone, sat at a breakfast table in Mammoth Hot Springs and said, "Let's build." The train tracks were built from St. Anthony, Idaho and the first train arrived in West Yellowstone, in 1908. Bud lived there just 26 years after E.H. came through.

Even today, the shortest way from West Yellowstone to Lakeview is about 30 miles on a dirt road. Little did Bud know that years hence, we would be telling his story, covering his lonely hours, days, and months, his life during 1932, from those warm summer days to the early, cold wintery nights.

Bud, of course, a single guy in the middle of nowhere became lonely and on August 11, 1932, ended his letter with the following:

> *For Heavens sake write i.e. if you care to, and let me know if you are sick, well, happy or sad or what not. As Ever, Bud*
>
> *P.S. I still think the same about you.*

There must have been a battle of who could ask for letters the most, as when I relate Beulah's letters later, she is also telling him to write more. I guess, a sign of mutual love.

Bud mentions at least three different times how lonesome he was. On May 29, 1933, he wrote, "*I am lonesome for a certain girl.*" And "*I traveled this long lonesome road.*" I could not help but think of the song in Seven Brides for Seven Brothers, "I'm a Lonesome Polecat." When he was writing to Beulah after they were married and had kids, he said, "I can't help thinking, *'My Dreams are Getting Better all the Time,'*" as in the song that Doris Day sang. Beulah also referred to that song in her letters.

Then, jumping the gun a little to the other side of the coin, Beulah shares in a letter dated Aug. 28, 1933, a bit of a chiding.

> *Are you really coming to see me? I could hardly believe my eyes when I read that. I haven't seen you for so long I was beginning to think I didn't rate anymore, as it says in the song "Absence makes the heart grow fonder"—of somebody else.*

It is strange how we can remember some applicable songs so long.

Bud must have had a fun, quick wit, as you will see. Dancing was the main form of entertainment. In one letter May 7, 1932, Bud told Beulah:

> *I was in West Yellowstone last night, after I did my shopping, I went to the dance. If a certain girl had been there with me, I could have had a good time.*

She chided him a little for going. He wrote back to her on July 21, with the following:

> *So, you think I go to Yellowstone quite often. Why of course I do. I have a summer girl there. Didn't you know that? She surely is a peach. She is 39 yrs. old, has a glass eye, a wooden leg, wears a wig, hump in her back, her front teeth are out, knock kneed and pigeon toes-, but along with all that, you're sure willing to believe everything that you hear! Now, don't believe all that I just wrote.*

Dancing was a major form of entertainment in those days. Ironic as it may seem, one of the few dancing places in West Yellowstone was the Tepee Bar. When Linda and I bought the Tepee from the Clawson's it was a bar and dance floor. We turned the dance floor into the red side of Three Bear Restaurant. Many times, I have heard of people coming to West Yellowstone and dancing at the Tepee. If those walls could talk, wouldn't it be ironic, if Bud came to the Tepee, to the dance that caused Beulah to get jealous? Especially, since it is now owned by their daughter Linda and her husband, Clyde.

Beulah and Bud were married on November 4, 1933, in Twin Falls Idaho. In a letter dated October 18, 1933, Bud wrote,

> *I'll be there next Fri. morning, better have your things ready for we shall leave as soon as I can get out of town. I'll have to stop at the bank for a little while . . . I guess your mother will say, yes, when I get there. I don't suppose she will feel so good when you go, do you? Say, maybe you thought it didn't take some courage to tell Dad what I intended to do. He didn't know just what to say . . . Hoping to have a couple arms full of love soon.*

We learned just today that Beulah's 95-year-old nephew was there when Bud came to pick up Beulah. He was dressed to the hilt and Beulah was all dressed up. They said their good-byes and got in the car and left.

I will close this section of Bud's letters with one dated Nov.10, 1933. In just 6 days after being married, he was back to work for his dad in Lakeview, alone again. He began his letter with "Darling . . . Say what is this about you that makes a fellow so lonesome when he is away?" —and ended it with "Your loving husband." I would have liked to include the whole letter but will leave some of that to your imagination. However, he talks a little about his dad.

Let me divert here to talk about the relationship of Bud and his dad, Ed. In the 1930 edition of the school yearbook, theTattler, Bud is pictured with the Ag Club. At the bottom it says, "The Agriculture Club is very proud of one of its members, Harry Fischer, who won the scholarship to the University of Idaho." Well, it never happened. Linda had always heard that "Bud's" dad used the money and wouldn't let him go to school. Instead, he was working with his dad on a cattle ranch at Lakeview with little income.

Bud's dad's first wife, passed away in January of 1931, just a few months after Bud graduated from High School. At the time Bud was working with his dad, another lady was mentioned and Bud did not care for her. Finally, and somewhat relieved, in one letter he said, his dad took the *"Lady of the Lake"* to see her mother and *"left her there."* Ed eventually married again to Dell and everyone loved her.

Imagine, wanting to go to school, winning a scholarship and then not being allowed to go, partly because of money. In a letter, dated June 5, 1932, he writes:

> *Dearest Beulah, I suppose Hugh Hill has returned from college by now; also the students from Utah and other places. Wish we were among them, don't you? I think that we have been handed a cold* (can't make out word), *but I guess it is all O.K. Let's not complain, things could be much worse for both of us.*

They must have both wanted to go to college but couldn't afford it. Linda and I both thought, how sad? But then Bud's positive comeback was, *Let's not complain. Things could be worse.* Beulah couldn't afford to attend college either as she was only making $3.00 per day.

When it was time for Linda to go to college, Beulah helped her financially, even though she was a single mom and had to take care of her own living expenses. Linda also worked by typing for 25 cents an hour.

It was also the goal of my family for all five kids to graduate from college and become teachers. All the family proceeds went to pay for each other's schooling. What a difference it would have made if Linda and I did not have our families support?

Now, why would I want to read a bunch of 91-year-old letters? Because of the mystery in a treasure chest of missing information about Linda's parents dating years. We have become intrigued readers of these 1932-1933 letters before their marriage and the 1945 letters after. I have been hungry to find out things that Linda did not even know, in order to get on paper, things that once were a protected secret. With time, such things become family history gems that should be recorded as part of family history. Such things could long be forgotten, if not written down.

I can empathize with Bud and his letter writing to Beulah. While Linda taught school in Anaheim, California for nine long months, I was anxious for her letters and I suppose like Bud, was looking for encouraging words of endearment from her.

There is so much more that could be written from Bud's letters, so let me give you my synopsis of what I learned.

Bud's school transcripts showed he was an intelligent person. For a man, he had beautiful penmanship and composed well-put-together letters. He wrote these letters with a steel nib dip pen on what is now 91-year-old paper. The letters were preserved so they looked like they had just been opened.

I have only recorded a few snippets of these newly found letters. They were not only intriguing regarding their personal relationship, but also of the workaday world they lived in. They made do and were content with the simple things of life.

I will refer back to Bud's letters periodically, at appropriate places later in the book. Now I will leave Bud's 1932-33 letters to Beulah behind, but not forgotten, and will record snippets of her letters to Bud in her section. I will also save Bud's 1945 letters to Beulah, after they became parents of Norman and Linda, sharing those in her section. They have given new meaning to the life of Linda's dad, Bud, for which we will be eternally grateful. For me, who never knew Bud in mortality, now I speak with Linda often about new things we know about them and the things that continually endear her parents to us. I am so deeply indebted to them for the "sweetheart" (see Bud is rubbing off on me already) I have now lived with for over 60 years.

Beulah Young

Beulah Young Fischer

Beulah Young was born November 6, 1912 in Twin Groves, Idaho to Stillman and Jenny Young and died April 10, 2007, at age 94. She was the youngest of seven children. Her siblings included Faunt, Myrtle, Lester, Blanche, Eunice, and Cyrus.

Beulah met Harry (Bud) Fischer during high school and fell head over heels for him. They were married on November 4, 1933, by a justice of the peace in Twin Falls, Idaho. She was 21, two days shy of 22 years old. Jokingly, it has always been said that they got married on the 4th and had Linda on the 5th.

I guess Beulah was like the swans at the Railroad Ranch, where they worked and lived when Linda was a little girl. Swans are abundant also in Yellowstone. They mate for life. When Beulah lost her mate, she was only 45 years old. After the death of Bud, she just never seemed interested in pursuing other romantic relationships. Linda and others asked Beulah why she never dated again. She said, "I had the best, why settle for something less." She was single for 50 years.

Beulah never liked her name. Years ago, in the 1950 era, there was a TV show called "The Beulah Show." Someone was always calling out in a high-pitched tone, Be-u'la. She probably didn't know that her name is found in Isaiah 62:4 and means 'married' and she stayed that way for 49 years, even though Bud was no longer with her.

We have also wondered where they came up with the name. One of Beulah's sisters is named Eunice. We lived in Twin Groves Ward with her. Here is my hypothesis as to why these two names were chosen by their parents.

In Wilford Woodruff's book, "Leaves from my Journal", page 51, he tells of his half-sister, Eunice Woodruff, who was teaching school there. He also mentioned he had just visited the grave of his mother, Bulah Woodruff, who died in 1808.

Notice that Bulah is spelled differently than our Beulah. Few people were revered more than the prophet, and Stillman and Jenny could have known and liked those contemporary names. President Woodruff died four years after Beulah was born.

Hence, isn't it possible that Stillman and Jenny named two of their daughters after the Woodruff names?

Beulah always worked and had many different jobs over the years, such as the Ashton grocery store, Bank of Commerce, potato warehouse in Rexburg, to name a few. She worked for the cleaners in Ashton and when the owner was called up to serve in the Korean War, he asked if she would run the place while he was gone. She was always a conscientious worker and was a pleasant person to be around.

Twenty-one years after Linda was born to Bud and Beulah, I wonder what Beulah thought as I picked her precious daughter up and took Linda to the temple to be married? Little did Beulah know that Linda was also marrying into a new family, and future family, that would love and worship Beulah till her dying day.

Hot Rod Granny

"Hot Rod Granny," was the name she will always be remembered by with her grandkids. When we bought Three Bear Lodge, we were open in the summer and closed in the winter. She came to help us out in the summer and live in our OSL 150 rail car then back to the little house we owned in St. Anthony for the winter.

The railroad car was accessed by a dirt road, past the big water tower. The kids would love it when they would ride with her. She would get the kids in her green Pinto and hunch over the steering wheel, step on the gas, make reeving sounds and swerve back and forth, saying "Here comes Hot Rod Granny." The kids got a kick out of it as she would drive them to get root beer floats, etc. And "Hot Rod Granny" stuck, as she was still driving into her 80's.

Beulah was always happy to have the kids stay with her when we went tripping. When they would stay with her in St. Anthony, there was always a black trunk that they weren't allowed to get into and a green jar with a bunch of change in it that they were. Hack's little grocery store was just next door, and they could take a few coins and buy penny candy. Or she would drive them to Rexburg and take them to Taco Time, her favorite. Strange, how little memories of her wit and kindness become memories that linger for a lifetime.

Mike said one thing he always remembered about Grandma was her stories she loved to tell. She was a great storyteller. I remember her telling us about when she worked in the potato factory. She also shared about going to see movies at the theater when she was a girl. I always liked hearing stories about Grandpa (Bud) because we were never able to meet him.

Some years ago, Linda had said of Beulah:

> *After we had been in West Yellowstone for a couple years and we had our first daughter, Rochelle, she could see that it was pretty hard for us to have a family and run a very demanding and time-consuming business. She was willing to move to West Yellowstone for the summers and help us out. She was a BIG help. In fact, I don't know how we could have done it all without her. She would tend the kids while I worked and then she worked at Three Bear while I was at home.*
>
> *This was the beginning of a beautiful and tender loving relationship between a grandmother and her grandkids, which remains to this day. For a long time, it was just Rochelle and Stephanie, and in her eyes, they could do no wrong. And this has never changed to this day. Then Mike, Brook and Doug came along, and it was the same thing. This, however, brought a challenge as she now had to worry about boy things like BB guns, snowboards, 4-wheeler, camping in the woods and she was always concerned for their safety. She now had 5 PERFECT grandkids which became the light of her life. They in turn returned that love.*

Beulah was like her brothers, politicians to the core. She was very adamant about her views and didn't mind espousing them. She always knew what the politicians were doing wrong and was rather openly critical about the bloopers they would make. This all added to her fun and feisty personality. She was likable on the front desk of the motel and knew how to deal with people. She was the mainstay of the operation.

It was while she was at the front desk that many people got to know her. After her passing we received many cards. Here are a some quotes:

> *She was always the exemplary "Grandmother," a sunny person in a sometimes-cloudy world. She added a beautiful dimension to our lives, and we shall miss her.*

Another:

> *She was a super lady. I always enjoyed visiting with her and admired her attitude and spunk as she grew older.*

While we thought we were getting a good deal by having her work for us, we didn't know how much she would impact our lives at the time. For you see, we had not only a built-in babysitter but a grandma all of us formed a loving relationship with, who's memory is indelibly imprinted in all our lives. This established a close and loving relationship between her and our kids. While we were closed in the winter, we could take our little Rochelle and later even our older kids to spend a week or two with her. The kids all looked forward to staying with Grandma or having her stay with them.

She was our "peace of mind" person which made Linda and I feel comfortable traveling. First, we loved to ski and could go to Jackson and later Big Sky. Then, Linda and I decided to travel by ourselves in the fall and vacation with our kids in the spring. As a couple, we were able to go to Italy, Europe, Hawaii, Caribbean and quite a few other cruises. We went to Ireland, Nassau, England, Australia and South Africa all up until 2005 when she got old enough to cause us to worry.

Linda has often talked about her parents' relationship. As was mentioned earlier, Bud was stern when it came to table manners and being respectful to their mom and grandparents. Neither Beulah nor he were given to show much affection toward each other. They were not flamboyant in expressing or showing love and affection to each other in the open.

Linda has always talked about the matter-of-fact relationship between her dad and mom. She never saw her dad and mom kiss or express love or make flirtatious gestures. But that may have been pretty normal then.

Bud was a down-to-earth business guy and didn't show much affection outwardly. They knew he loved them, but that word never came from his mouth. It was a relaxed and happy homelife but long after Bud's passing, Linda commented many times that even though her parents never said they were loved, she still knew they were.

Bud never used affectionate nicknames, or so we thought, like "darling" or "sweetheart" etc. Physical touching or mentioning love in the first person was shared at a minimum, at least while their kids were around. But, after 90 years, we found out the exciting, "rest of the story."

After Beulah died, we rented the house to Bill Edgington, Beulah's nephew and Linda's cousin. He pretty much just moved in and kept Beulah's things in a back room. Beulah must have put Bud's and her things, and other keepsakes, in the trunk pictured below. It was a safe place where those things of a personal nature could be kept.

What happened to the trunk in the meantime? How did it get here?

When Bill moved out, he brought a plastic tote full of Beulah's things and the trunk to us. We just thought we would get around to looking in the trunk sometime, but 'out of sight, out of mind,' as the saying goes and we just never got around to it.

So, there it was hiding in plain sight. It was sitting against the wall in Brook and London's room for 14 years. I have helped Linda make the beds in that room for all those years. How could an old trunk of Linda's parents just sit all that time, seen, but no one ever just lifted the lid?

Mysteries of life within "The Trunk"

About a week ago, when Brook was here, Linda suggested that we look in the trunk. It was like opening a time capsule that had been closed for 90 years.

But first, the younger generation may not even know what a travel trunk is. The photo above is the actual one belonging to Bud and Beulah. This one was made of thin plywood on the inside and covered with thin metal on the outside. It was then reinforced around the edges with more metal and corner protective brackets that protruded enough to add strength to protect corners and edges. Originally, trunks were made for long travel and kept for storage later.

When I was growing up, I also remember a trunk where Mother stored clothing not currently being used. Her fur coat, linen tablecloths, and seasonal clothing were folded neatly inside. In those days closets were a luxury and to conserve space, clothing, valuable things and keepsakes were stored therein. It was moth proof and had a separate layered compartment to separate smaller keepsakes. I can imagine trunks being brought across the plains because they were so durable and would keep the dust out.

Trunks have been used around the world for thousands of years. The small, flat-topped trunk, like Beulah's, was used for extended travel trips. They also served a long-term practical purpose, storage of keepsakes. For security, they normally have a rather strong lock.

North Americans use the term "trunk" because until 1930 most drivers used to strap travel chests, called trunks, to the backs of their car. Once the car makers started incorporating built-in rear compartments, trunks, there was no longer any reason to use them.

Now that we have had a refresher course on what trunks are, let me tell you more about Beulah's old black trunk. It sat for years in the back bedroom of her house in St. Anthony. When Rochelle and Stephanie were young girls, they often asked if they could look in her trunk. The answer was always an emphatic, "No." Later, the boys remembered it being put in the basement and they often asked if they could look inside but she always said something to pass it off. It just seemed to be off limits. Linda reminded me that she grew up with that trunk all her home life. She also asked her mother if she could see what was in the trunk, especially after Bud died. Her mother just passed it off and said, "No, it is just old stuff that you wouldn't be interested in." Or "No, not today," and other times just, "No!" Little did Linda know how much its contents would change her appreciation for her dad and mom.

As indicated earlier, Bill had brought the trunk and a plastic tote to us years ago. We put it in an upstairs bedroom and pretty much ignored it. So, there it was hiding in plain sight. It was sitting against the wall in Brook and London's room for 14 years. All those years, I helped Linda make the beds in that room. How could an old trunk of Linda's parents just sit all that time, seen, but no one ever lifted the lid?

A few days ago, when Brook was here, and Linda was looking for something to do, she asked him to bring out the old black trunk so they could look in it. Stephanie and our grandson Drake also got involved. What would we find? Would there be any love letters inside? Would there be things about her dad that we had never known? What was it that caused Beulah not to let her daughter and grandkids look inside? Would we find out things about Beulah that we had never known before? It was like opening up a time capsule with the expectation of finding treasures there. Well, there were treasures inside alright, not nuggets of silver and gold, but things more precious. There were things that tugged at our hearts and answered so many questions. In the interest of space, I will mention only a few of the nuggets we found inside. But why did we not open the trunk 14 years ago?

Many times in our lives we receive promptings to do things. I have felt prompted to write this biography, with ongoing promptings many times in the process. In this instance, I am of the belief, uncanny as it may be, that it was just the opposite.

Could it be that it was just never meant to be opened earlier? Could it be that a *stupor of thought* fell on us until Linda was prompted to get the trunk out to see what was inside?

If it had been opened by inquisitive grandchildren, or even Linda and I years ago, things would have been trifled with, lost or left in disarray. Instead, things were placed as Beulah had left them. Also, I was not writing Linda's biography then and it would not have had the impact as it has now. It couldn't have been timelier. Even after I started to write, at just the right time, a whole new insight into her parent's life opened to us.

It was exciting to open the trunk. We lifted the lid and saw for the very first time things that had not been seen in many years. There were six of Bud's rodeo trophies, his Catholic study books, lots of pictures, and an old newspaper, dated December 22, 1931. According to the ads, you could buy dresses for $1.00, with sizes up to 52. Men's suits were $12.95. And you could purchase beautiful occasional chairs for $3.98.

One of the first treasures we found was a handwritten sketch of the life of Beulah Young Fischer. It was written by her mother, Jenney Young, in her own handwriting with a pencil. I will share that sketch here, skipping details of dates and genealogical things that are recorded elsewhere. I will, however, include those things that were written by Beulah's mother before Linda was born. I will share it as written, including her spelling, but will add some punctuation. I chose to keep it unique to her and indicative of the education at the time. Few people went beyond the 8th grade and many not even that far. Beyond these errors, inside this sketch, is the warm and caring heart Jenney Young had for her family, which is not to be lost.

Skitch of the life of Beulah Young Fischer
(written by her mother)

Beulah Young Fischer was Born 6 Nov. 1912 in Twin Groves, Fremont co. Idaho at the old family home where her parents had lived ever since they war married in 1894.

Childhood memorys

Beulah had an adventure while going thru natinl Park, had picture taken with wild Bears, seen a Band of wild Elk, also Buffalo. went all on the Boards walks in Noris Baison, frightened her mother many times as she went to close to the gisers fed old Jessie James the grizzly Bear some fruit.

(Accidents) was thrown from the jints strides or swing at school. was in a car when a forty was shivering and the car was tiped over.

Was of medium size had soft wavy Brouwn Hair and eyes, wait about 120 lbs, was a sunny dispersion and very Ambisous and very tidy and clean in body and dress, new how to make a home-could sew, good cook make Butter culd help her Father milk the cows could wride a horse good. Loved a good show, to dance, swim, play Basket Ball. Culd drive and handle a car, loved to travel had 2 ambitions. As a small child was loved and petted by all the family being the baby of a family of seven girls and boys. She loved real good Books and admired girls and boys with high Ideals and kind regards for older people. Was a leader among her friends and after she was married she was anxious to help her husband to make thir way in the world have lived in Idaho and Montana and thir home was blessed with a little son on Aug. 23, 1936. Thay named him Norman Foster Fischer. She took pride in doing all her own sewing and was proud of her beautiful boy with his big brown eyes and Red hair. She was alwa truthful and had a great love for her parents also reverard the lives of her grandparents as they were pineers and helped to subdue this western country her grandmothers culd spin and weave the cloth for the cloth for their familys.

Then there was what we had hoped for: several bundles of letters held together in groups by rubber bands, old and brittle.

We organized them into three groups. One was written by Bud to Beulah, during the summers and early winter of 1932 and 1933, while he was working at Lakeview, Montana. The second group was written by Beulah to Bud from St. Anthony during the same time period. Then there was the third group of 16 letters, even more "mushy," that were written by Bud to Beulah, 12 years after being married. These were written in 1945, where he often talked about how lonely he was, how he missed his family and about typical everyday happenings.

Even though the 1945 letters are from Bud, I will include them under Beulah's tribute as they are more applicable to the family.

Before writing about the letters, however, I will mention the senior yearbooks from St. Anthony High School's *Tatler*. This was the same school I attended some 27 years later, and I still cherish my *Tatler*, from my senior year in 1957. It is with a joyous but heavy heart, words that are not often used together, that I relate to you the feelings Linda had as we eventually read the autographs at the front of Beulah's and Bud's senior yearbooks. We learned things that, in a way, caused her to be happy and yet sad.

First, we read from Bud's 1930 *Tatler* yearbook. We were both surprised to read in the short autographs from classmates and well wishes, things we had not known before. We did not know that Bud received the Citizenship Cup. Fourteen people commented on this in the yearbook and told him he deserved it. Twelve people wished him well in his upcoming college years. It said in the yearbook he had received a scholarship to University of Idaho. (However, as mentioned elsewhere, he was not able to attend because of his dad.) He was a tackle on the football team and many comments were made about his ability. Under his senior photo it said, "Everybody likes Harry "Bud" especially the girls."

Apparently, this was the transition time when he received the nickname "Bud" because most people still referred to him as "Harry."

As mentioned, we recently found in the second treasure trove (tote) a newspaper article entitled, *"HARRY FISCHER WINS SCHOLARSHIP."*

I will quote only the part that deals with Bud.

> *In extra-curricular activities, Harry Fischer has had a prominent part. He has been on the St. Anthony football team for four years, was two years president of the Future Farmers club, won first place in the stock judging contest at the Blackfoot fair, won the best stockman up in 1929, is a member of the calendar and finance committee of*

the high school, is vice-president of the student body, and a member of the 1930 Tatler staff.

In addition to his extracurricular activities Harry has kept a good scholarship record. He is pleasant, industrious, likable and will certainly prove deserving for this honor. He plans to take up the scholarship and enter the university next fall.

Apparently, he did much more than just attend school. He was very active in more than just scholastic requirements.

Next is Beulah's 1931 *Tatler* yearbook. Beulah was on the debate team and eight people commented on that. That surprised us greatly, but if the debates were on politics, not so much. (When she was with us, she seemed willing to have a sporadic debate regarding politics at the drop of a hat.) She was referred to as the "sweetest girl," seven times. She was wished success in college four times. She had indicated she wanted to take classes in bookkeeping. But since she had to attend to an ailing mother and because they couldn't afford it, she was never able to attend.

As mentioned above Linda was both happy and also a little *mad* that she never knew any of these things about her parents. I suppose they probably thought the kids wouldn't be interested in their youth. Perhaps this should be a lesson to all, that even though sometimes our kids don't seem to care or may seem bored, time endears the memory of things in our family. For eighty plus years, Linda would have loved to have known such things about her parents.

Though we don't know when Bud and Beulah began to date, they obviously knew each other well during school. Bud graduated in 1931 and the letters began in 1932, so a romance must have developed between high school and his working at Lakeview Montana.

Now, back to the letters. Not only was it interesting to learn things about Bud and Beulah that we had not known before, it was interesting to learn about the lifestyle that is so foreign to the youth of today. As I have already written, Bud became more loveable and understandable to Linda, and almost like a living, caring person to me, a person I would dearly love to have known.

Remembering causes us to preserve the memory.

Let me tell you some of the secrets we found in Beulah's letters. Well, not secrets, just enlightenment on a softer relationship that none of us knew. I feel like I am walking on a little thin ice here by sharing what we found in Beulah's letters. She was a very private person in many ways, and the letters I am going to talk about were kept in the trunk for a reason. However, the "statute of limitations" has run out, and perhaps, especially after all these years, they are now in the "public domain." Apart from all the legal jargon, we are family and want to preserve their stories for future generations.Beulah must have read and reread those letters in the 51 years after Bud had passed away and knew that someday they would be in our care and keeping. Perhaps it was a way of letting her posterity know how much she cherished their love, since she was so protective of it. But knowing Beulah, I may pay for it, like our son Mike said, "I remember one time we were messing around and Michelle called in reinforcements to back her up. Next thing you know, here comes grandma and starts spanking her 30-year-old grandson."

It is interesting to dig into an old trunk and reconstruct a "love story." (Remember the 1970 movie with that same name starring Ali MacGraw and Ryan O'Neal? Another movie could well be made of the "Love Story" starring Beulah Young and Bud Fischer using the same theme song, only written in the early 1930's.)

It is almost unbelievable to even consider the lifestyle changes from then to 2023, ninety-one years ago. What did they do for entertainment? Why couldn't they just call each other on the phone? The old-fashioned kind was not even available then. Today, from kids to the elderly, we constantly carry a personal phone and 'Siri' brings a world of instant information to us. How did they get along without Facetime, or texting, or traveling in a comfortable car the one-hour distance to fix the 80 miles which separated them? What, no T.V.? Sorry, it had just been invented, but not available.

On the other hand, if they would have texted these "love" letters, we would have nothing that preserved their memory. As the heading, shared earlier, indicates, "Remembering causes us to preserve the memory." That is what Linda and I would like to accomplish now by writing our observations, for not only us, but for future generations.

Bud, as mentioned above, was in Lakeview, Montana. He had already told Beulah he would like to see her in his June 28, 1932 letter.

> *I would like to see you, but there are eighty miles between us isn't there? Well, I'll have to imagine I see you. I think about you a lot, how about you? Lots of love and a kiss, Bud.*

The first letter read of Beulah's was dated, Friday, June 17, 1932. She mentioned, "Hugh (a classmate) is home now. Honestly, I believe he has improved too. Maybe Moscow will be a great help to him, I hope so." (You may recall, Hugh was mentioned by Bud that he had been to University of Idaho, where Bud had won the scholarship, but couldn't attend because of his father.) Then with a little sense of humor she said:

> *I hear you were down last week and didn't even come and see me. Just how are you going to explain that? I really shouldn't have written after finding that out. Of course, though, I'm really very kind hearted. I'm not conceited, am I? . . . As ever, Beulah*

Aug 10th she wrote about the dances which were a main source of entertainment,

> *They have been having them at Warm River. I attend them all but not with a "date" . . . Gee, the radio is good tonight. Now don't that make you wish you were here? I love to hear popular songs and dance music and that is exactly the kind of a program we have right now.*

Finally, she signs off with "Love, Beulah." Then, with a note off to the side and an arrow pointing to 'love' she added, "Do you like the way I closed this letter?" Finally, after who knows how many letters and weeks later, she also signs off the way Bud did.

In another letter she says, "Now, you see if you were here, you could go and dance with me. (I'll bet you're glad you're not here)." Later in a letter, Beulah said they had a dance in Warm River, a dance at Ponds Lodge Monday, and another on Saturday. Dancing, movies, rodeos and listening to the radio seemed to be the main things for entertainment.

Pictured above is a newspaper advertisement of a 1930s car, though it is likely Bud or Beulah would have driven an older model. Notice the selling point, *a Smooth Ride on any Road*. To get to those places in their old automobiles would have been quite a trip from St. Anthony considering that at the time many roads were rough and unpaved.

Now I can empathize with their letter writing. Linda taught school in Anaheim, California for nine long months. One of the reasons I am intrigued about these letters is because I can empathize with Bud.

As mentioned under Bud's section, there must have been a battle going on as to who could ask for letters the most. On Aug. 6, 1933, Beulah wrote, "Talk about me being poor letter writer! Really though, why haven't you written to me? I've been looking for a letter from you every day for the last two weeks." Then she wanted him to come down to the rodeo and dance at Twin Groves. (I remember the dances and the rodeo grounds at Twin Groves. The dances continued, but the rodeo grounds were eventually turned into a ball field.)

On Aug, 16, Beulah says, "You must go to West Yellowstone quite often. I hear that it is a good town to have fun in. Now don't tell me you never step out? I heard you were going to have another rodeo up there the 4th of next month."

I suppose this is what triggered Bud's hilarious response mentioned earlier, about a girlfriend that was 39, glass eye etc.

It is interesting for us to speculate as to where Bud danced in West Yellowstone. There were a few bars at the time, but the Tepee Inn and Bar had a dance floor. Dancing was one of the main forms of entertainment and Bud would drive the 30 miles to West Yellowstone to do so.

The Tepee Inn was built by Paul & Dorothy Strieder in 1919.

The Tepee was a large two-story log structure built in 1919 that housed a bar, dance floor, cafe, and rooms. The original owner, Paul Strieder died in the early 1920s and later his wife, Dorothy, married Val Buchanan and continued to operate the hotel.

Lobby of the TePee Inn, 1934

As has been mentioned, Linda's dad would come to West Yellowstone to the dances in 1932. Little did he know that a generation later, his daughter would own the very property on which he danced.

The Tepee Inn was purchased in 1978 and remodeled to become
Three Bear Restaurant and Grizzly Lounge in 1984

After Bud's dancing days, the Tepee was sold to J.H. Venable and then to A.K. Clawson in 1952. Linda and I, along with Bill and Corole Howell, purchased the Tepee from Clawson on May 25, 1978. Later, we bought out Carole and Bill, and they continued to lease the space for the new Grizzly Lounge.

I reported on the letter from Bud to Beulah earlier about him picking her up for the wedding. They were married November 4,1933. They came back from their wedding and returned to their jobs nine days later. Beulah writes: "Dearest Bud: Thought I better write and tell you that we have about decided to have a dance. I know you won't like it but my family insists. You can stand it though if I can." I suppose this would be a dance for them as they were married in Twin Falls.

One of the early houses that Bud and Beulah lived in is on the north side of highway 287 and Henry's Lake. Beulah always pointed out, when we would drive by, that she lived there for a time, after their marriage. We recently came across a photo of this little house, that was a gift to us and had been professionally framed. On the back it states. "Beulah's cabin at Henry's Lake, Temporary home of Bud, Beulah, and Norman—1937, still standing today."

Temporary home of Bud, Beulah and Norman

Pictured above is the cabin, years after Bud and Beulah lived there. It was much younger then, but still old and abandoned. Over the years we have watched this cabin as age has crept up on it. Eventually, the roof caved in, then the rafters and side log walls began to rot and disintegrate. The photo on the right shows its almost burial in the deep snows of 2023. This also gives an idea of the snow Bud would shovel off to prevent roofs from caving in when he worked at the Railroad Ranch.

Love letters normally stop after a marriage, but not with Bud and Beulah. There is a gap in the timeline after their marriage in 1933, but the trail of letters picks up again in 1945, after Norman and Linda had arrived on the scene and Bud worked at the Railroad Ranch.

It is my belief, through these letters and memories of Linda and her cousin, Sally Young Webster, that Bud worked for the Maglebys on a ranch just south of Henry's Lake, Idaho. It was here, when Sally's dad, Uncle Cy caught a 17.5 pound, 35.5-inch-long trout in Duck Creek (Photo in Twinkle #1). This was around 1941. Little Linda and Cousin Sally drug the other fish they caught in a landing net up to the cabin in which they lived, next to an old Pullman railroad car that was nearby.

From Maglebys, Linda and her family lived at Herriman's Railroad Ranch in the summer, where they lived in the cookhouse. Linda was too young to attend school, but she remembers Norman having to do schoolwork at home. Her dad would not let her go down to the barn for any reason. Later, her mother said the cows were having calves and he did not want her to see that. (Which was similar to my dad that wouldn't let my cousin Connie go to the sheep shed, where the sheep were lambing.)

The next winter, because Linda was old enough to attend school, the family moved down to Ashton. Bud spent a long, lonely winter feeding cattle and shoveling snow that was 5-6 feet deep at the Railroad Ranch. Hence the following letters, written in 1945. It was during this winter that he wrote the 16 letters that we treasure now.

From here on, however, it was like listening to a one-sided conversation. Bud's letters to Beulah were kept, but no letters were kept from Beulah to him.

Before continuing with specific letters, perhaps it would be well to fill in a few overall details. Since the letters stopped, I assume so did Bud's employment at Lakeview. I felt like a defective detective as I read through the letters after they were married. There were no envelopes with these, just the letters folded with no post office and no date stamp. On one letter was written 1/21/45, the rest were for instance, Feb. 4- or Sun. -11. I had to compare dates and days with a 1945 calendar to get a sequence.

Sixteen Lonely Letters

Well, I've left the suspense hanging long enough. In the letters, hiding in the trunk, written by Bud to Beulah in 1945, he refers to 'mushy' things quite often.

1/7/45

> "*Dearest Beulah and kids: Just thought I would say hello and how are you? Have you missed me since I came back? I'll bet not.*" Then he goes on with mundane marriage things like, "*did you pay the income tax for $45.20. Seems like quite a lot.*" He wanted to know about Messa, his filly that he wanted to get registered and later became his rodeo horse. *Then, "Honey, I just don't seem to be able to think of anything to write, only a little mush and you wouldn't be interested in that, I know.*"

So, sixteen letters were sent in which, at first, we were most interested in reading the 'mushy stuff,' (his words) because it tells us of their love for each other that was never expressed openly. I will be careful to keep out of their bedroom relationship and will only talk of things I hope they wouldn't mind me telling to our posterity, those things that today would not be uncommon for couples to talk about more openly.

In the letters hiding in the trunk, written in 1945, he refers to 'mushy' things quite often.

1/15, the second letter starts out.

> "*My dear, Darling, Sweetheart: Beulah: Please disregard the mush as it is above, I don't mean it as you can tell. It ends with, Good night dearie and tell the kids hello. Why don't you write a note to Dad and thank him for the presents and tell them how the kids like their things,*

he wants to know how Linda liked the Mex. doll. Here are a couple of kisses. Bud"

1/21/45

"Dearest Beulah & kids: Well you missed a mail day-no letter. Surely you have time to write at least three times a week to your poor lonesome husband. . . . Last night it was -10 degrees and tonight it will be colder, wish you were here to keep me warm these cold nights."

It doesn't appear that Bud ever left the ranch in that whole winter. He was continually requesting things be brought in (that we take for granted today). He wrote and asked Beulah the following:

Jan. 11

"I wish you would come up to see me. I would be awfully nice to you. Probably would even let you sleep in my bed, provided you would wear your 'see more' gown." Then he asked if she could send up *"some of those bitter sweet Hersey Bars and some Kodak film size A-8."* On Feb. 8, he wrote: *"Honey, Caroline would like you to bring two bunches of celery and a small squash, if you should come up Sunday. I have already told you what I want. Be sure to send me some stamps to send letters. I don't like to send them collect. I may want to write to a girlfriend somewhere besides Ashton."*

It is my understanding that mail only came up twice a week and I'm now sure when the roads were plowed throughout the winter.

Feb-1

"my Dear Beulah and kids: Guess I better write to my honey before I go to bed, as you insisted that I write every mail day." (Mail came twice a week) *". . . I just don't*

know what to do about this place. There are four of us
and only enough work for 3 until spring anyway."

He goes on to say that he is concerned about not having a job
and that he would be stuck for the army. (He mentions throughout
these letters, that he may be drafted as World War II was still going
on but ended the next summer.) "Maybe I can get a job with some
sheep outfit to feed for next winter."

That made me chuckle, as Linda's Uncle Les teased her about her
dad being a "sheep herder." Also, then he said, "Maybe we could be
together next winter, if I am not called up . . ." Do you think you are
worth this much to me, to have me work on a farm for someone, you
would sure have to turn on a lot of loving, do you think you could
do that and keep it up for the rest of our lives, If I should consent to
live with you?"

Feb. 4

> *"My Dearest Beulah: Just thought I better write a few*
> *lines tonight and let you know how much I like to get*
> *your letters. Even if they aren't mushy like mine are. I*
> *just can't help but be a little bit silly about you." Then*
> *later, "Well my sugar plum, are you as sweet tonight as I*
> *think you are? . . . If you want me to write to you, I will*
> *need some more writing material and stamps," (He must*
> *write a lot as he often repeats this request.) "I'll close for*
> *this time and hope you all are OK, I am. Tell the kids*
> *hello for me and tell Norman to work hard in school and*
> *Linda to be a good girl. All my love to you, you know the*
> *rest honey and I mean it. Bud."*

Feb. 6 Bud writes about the deep snow and the wind has blown
the roads shut. He proposes a plan where she could come up to see
him and what he would do for her if she came. Then:

> *"Say, honey, if you don't want my bare to show, you better*
> *get busy about some bib overalls, for me W34" – L.30"*

mine are about shot. Well honey, I will close now and go to bed alone, no fun. Only to dream about, 'My dreams are getting better all the time' as the song goes . . . All of my love to you and the kids. Bring something to eat. Love Bud."

He had a rather small waist but had a larger stout chest and was strong enough to bulldog a steer.

Also, in those days, in the country, telephones were normally only available on what we called 'party lines,' where multiple people shared the line and could listen in on what others were saying. In his Feb. 8 letter he mentioned he didn't want to have Mrs. Clark listening in on what they said. Hence, I believe the reason for more letters.

On Jan 15, Bud wrote:

"I am sorry to know that you are sick. However, am glad that you called to let me know your better, at least temporarily. I sure hope that you get along all right. If you don't, be sure to call me, won't you . . . Say did Linda shed a few tears after she talked to me? She sounded like s(h)e was about to cry when she said goodbye. However, she wasn't the only one who was unhappy. That was the first time I ever talked to one of the kids over the telephone, you know.

I'll be darned if I know whether it is worthwhile, having a family in one place and me being another. You hardly know them if you ever do get to see them.

It takes something like this, to make a person realize what a family meant to you, I guess. If you don't want to work next week I wouldn't take chances, However, I guess the Dr. will advise you what to do. If you are feeling able you could even come up and stay a few days

next week if you don't think you better work. I think it
would be good idea anyway.

Did the stockings for Linda come with the order? I
sent three pair, if they came, you didn't mention it, so I
wondered. So, the things for you were OK. I am glad. I
just had to guess a size; you know.

I got a new (Montgomery) Wards catalog, sure are a lot of
nice things in it. I may send for some more things. I'll try
to get Norman something, there is a pair of shoes listed,
I think we should get him for every day. Well Honey, all
I can do for you is hope for the best, as long as I am up
here. Maybe things won't always be like they are now."

A little side note regarding the Wards catalog. If you did not live
where there was a local Montgomery Ward's store you could receive
their catalog and order all kinds of really nice things. There he was
in a remote location where the mail only came a couple times a week
and he could order through the mail. It would be like a 1940's version
of today's Amazon.

As kids, we used to look through the catalogs and wish for many
things. When a new one would come, we would take the old one out
to the outdoor privy and when it came the appropriate time, we would
tear out 1 or 2 pages, crinkle and stretch them out several times to
make them softer and use them for toilet paper. Perhaps that was the
beginning of recycling in my mind that was later replaced with the
Three Bear "white shirt" recycling program.

In the last letter, Bud mentioned Beulah being sick. This is the
next letter, and we find out why.

Feb. 20

"My Dearest Beulah and Kids: I was very much relieved
to hear that you were better, However, I am still a little
shaky to think what a close call that you had. You know
that is very serious to have the appendix burst, don't you

*let a pain like you had go again for it could be the last one
you know. I would like to consult with another Doctor.
However, Dr. Soule probably was correct. . . . Even tho
I wasn't there, I was very much worried over you. I may
not seem so concerned over your being sick but I really
was. You know how much I love you, don't you honey,
you are better anyway. I wish I could see you. I know you
would get well faster then. Love for now to you all. Bud"*

Linda remembers her mother being in the hospital when she was
little, and both she and I remember Dr. Soule, our family doctor in
St. Anthony.

His wish must have paid off because Bud must have been down to
see Beulah as in his Feb 27 letter, he says, "Better get back to the old
job again, writing three letters every week . . . Do you feel better now
honey? Now that I have been down to cheer you up, you should be
regaining your health faster. Do you feel better now I've been down?"

Sun 11

"My Darling Beulah:" Bud asks Beulah if she couldn't
come up and see him while she has time off work.
*"Norman could stay with Blanche while going to school.
You know I have to figure some way to get some loving
for you, else you will forget what it is like. Let me know
what you think of the idea, will you?"*

*"Thursday, March 20th, My dearest Beulah and Kids:
Thanks for the package, everything was great. Enjoyed
your letter so much. As you know, there are so many
things happening here that make news, I just can't find
the space on a sheet of paper to write about them."* He
goes on to talk about Beulah having to move and her
workaday world. He must have been upset with the
other three he worked with as he shared it would be
nice if all three of them would be gone for the rest of

the winter. About that he said, *"They don't bother me but irritates me to be this close to them so long. I know I shouldn't feel that way. However, if you were here this winter and I wasn't alone, I probably wouldn't have so much time to think about them."*

On March 12th, while Beulah was still recovering, we assume, he shared:

"Don't forget to ask the Dr. when I can sleep with you again. However, with your sore-tummy I know? How do they treat you now that you are a little better: . . . Say we are having a little bit of spring around here now. The snow has settled a good foot in the past few days. Lee had to break a new road with the caterpillar. We haven't had any trouble with the roads to speak of tho. Well honey, I will close now as I must go to bed and get my rest. Also, I go to bed alone . . . All my love to you and the kids. Tell them hello. Love, Bud."

In this letter, Bud also mentions a friend named Lee, whose wife, Caroline he had given some bananas. That was Lee and Caroline Jacobsen. I met Lee when he was the first West Yellowstone Branch President in The Church. I was 18 and he came out back of Three Bear where I was hanging sheets to dry on the line. He asked If I would be in charge of the Young Adult Program for the summer and organize both Sunday and weekly gatherings.

After Linda and I were married, Lee often told Linda how much he had liked Bud. Lee was the first Branch President in West Yellowstone for 11 years and I was the third for almost 14 years. It is strange how paths often cross.

Through reading these one-sided love letters from a lonely husband married for 11 years and then separated for a long, cold, deep winter at the Railroad Ranch, I reflect on my own marriage. At the time, Bud was about 33 years old. On the contrary, I am now 84 and Linda and I have only been separated for short periods of time. In

1980 she traveled for a week with the Western Airlines promotional winter trip, where she, along with about a dozen other ski operators, were marketing across the U.S. winter vacations. I used to do the same for years. But the longest we were separated was 10 days when I went to London's World Travel Market. I might add, we could not wait to get back into the loving arms of each other.

In bringing to an end the quotes I have chosen from the letters in the trunk, I have tried to give a flavor of the sentimental side of her parents, but have been careful not to go into things that I think are too private and personal.

I was told one time, about giving counsel to couples, to "stay out of the bedroom." I have tried to do that when quoting some of their letters. However, if you read between the lines, I can assure you, Bud was always respectful of what he said to Beulah.

Beulah's piercing eyes as I reveal her secret letters

While writing this section, I placed this photo about 3 ft. away from me. With her piercing eyes looking into mine, I was careful not to be disrespectful of their intimacy. For if I was, maybe like Mike said, she may come and spank her 80+ year old son-in-law.

Beulah kept these letters and other keepsakes and remembrances of Bud in a trunk for safe keeping for a reason. It is my belief that she kept those things private for many years, knowing that someday the things contained therein would be shared with her posterity. Some things we talk about openly, some things we don't.

It seems that Bud and Beulah each lived two separate lives and, in a sense, had two different sides of themselves living within each.

Perhaps this is true for most of us. The first is the side that we want everyone to know, the typical, public, work-a-day life where we try and put our best foot forward; the person that attends work, meetings, church and public-related daily activities. The second is the private, intimate relationship between husband and wife. It is ordained of God that we "go forth and multiply and replenish the earth." In order to preserve the sanctity of this relationship, those personal feelings and actions are to be kept private. In other words, I wanted to share enough to show the deep love they had for each other. In private, Bud used words of endearment freely in his letters to Beulah. Linda, who had never heard those words spoken between them, was so pleased to learn her father had shared such a love with her mother.

I must say that at first, we were anxious to see if there was any "mushy stuff" in the letters, as Bud referred to it often. Well, there was no short supply of that very thing. We were looking for those kinds of things because Linda had never known that side of her parents. Many times, she commented on how happy it made her feel to read about those tender and intimate times her parents shared. Norman never knew any of this during his life.

At the conclusion of my experience reading Bud's letters, I would like to pass on a few observations regarding my father-in-law. First, I was impressed with his handwriting on a lined 5"X 8" stationary tablet paper. His spelling, punctuation and paragraphs were consistently correct. He used the word "surely" a lot. So did many who wrote in his yearbooks. They must have had a very good English teacher. While "surely" is an adverb modifying a verb, "sure" is an adjective modifying a noun.

I think I have gotten lazy in my writing, "surely" has been replaced with just "sure." You will not find the word surely many times in my book. My bad.

But the thing that I was really impressed about was his lack of cross outs or corrections. In all his letters, I could not find one. His high school report card showed his grades were in the 80's and 90's, still quite good. Apparently, they didn't use A-F at that time. I can't tell you how many times, as I have been writing this book, I have crossed out or deleted and made corrections. I wish I were as articulate as Bud. The content of his letters, in addition to the "mush," were very caring, and considerate of Beulah's folks, the rest of her family, and others.

All the letters of Bud and Beulah and their keepsakes will now reside where we found them, in the trunk. Now they are clipped together with my sticky notes, marking parts that were referred to above. Hopefully, future generations will continue to find love and excitement as they look at these for the first time and read the treasure left by Bud and Beulah.

When putting the letters away, I found an old steel pen tip. Could this be what Bud wrote with in his letters to Beulah?

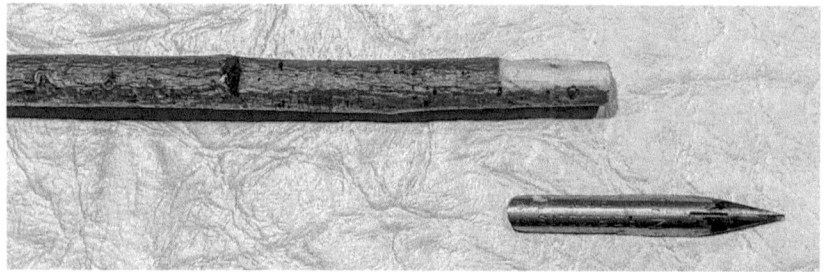

The steel pen tip was found in the trunk before
attaching the handle I made out of a willow.

It has been intriguing to notice the different modes of writing found in the trunk. We are able to see physical evidence of the progression of writing instruments. The invention of the ballpoint pen in the 1930s made the transfer of the written word much easier. However when Linda and I were little, the steel nib pen was still being used occasionally. In the 1930s, the ballpoint pen began to be widely used. Contained in the trunk were samples of different writing during that time. Bear with me as I pursue, as a sideline, the changes that only us older folks would remember using, or in fact, knew about.

Writing instruments through time

As mentioned, in the bottom of the trunk tucked away in a corner we found the tip of an old steel nib pen. I have not seen one since I was a kid. In reading Bud's letters, it was noticed that his writing would get dim in some places and then it darkens up again. He was probably using the steel pen shown above. When the little supply of ink in the pen tip was running out, one would dip it in the ink to make it dark again.

When we were kids in school there were holes in each desktop that held the little bottle of ink. Though they weren't used much by then, the holes were still there. When my mother wrote in each of our five baby books, she would use a dip pen and if we didn't have pen ink available, she would dip the pen into Mrs. Stewart's Liquid Bluing, which was used to whiten clothes. It was a little lighter but worked as well as regular dipping ink.

Finding the little metal pen tip tweaked my interest as to what tools people have used for writing throughout history. So, in checking into the different ways of writing, I found the evolution of the writing instruments interesting. With the help of Google I found the following:

The Quill pen (made from larger bird feathers) was popular for about 1500 years and was used by our country's forefathers. Thomas Jefferson bred special geese to keep himself equipped with writing implements. Because of their shape, only the five feathers at the tip of the left wing would do. Left-handers could use feathers from the right wing. Then a pen knife was used to cut and shape the feathers into nibs.

Incidentally, the words pen knife comes from a small knife that was used to thin and point quills for dip pens, called nibs. If you were lucky, your quill might last a week. Small wonder Britain imported twenty-seven million quills a year from Russia alone.

In 1803 the steel nib pen was patented. It became very popular when it began to be mass produced in Birmingham, England in 1822. Inside Beulah's trunk, a steel nib pen inscribed with "Perkins Pen No. 3. was found (shown here). . I made the handle out of a willow.

Mrs. Stewarts Bluing was what Mother used in her early writing. Look closely at the words written with this pen. Notice the light then dark writing.

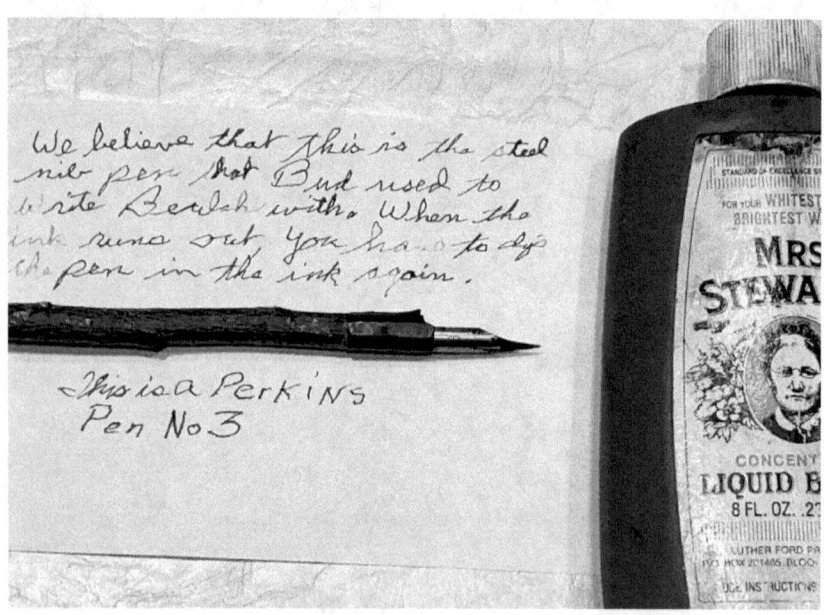

Example of dip pen writing: Notice the ink's darkness.

The metal nib was made of copper and bronze, while today, it is made of steel. It has a slit that leads the ink from a vent hole to the paper and works by a combination of gravity and capillary action.

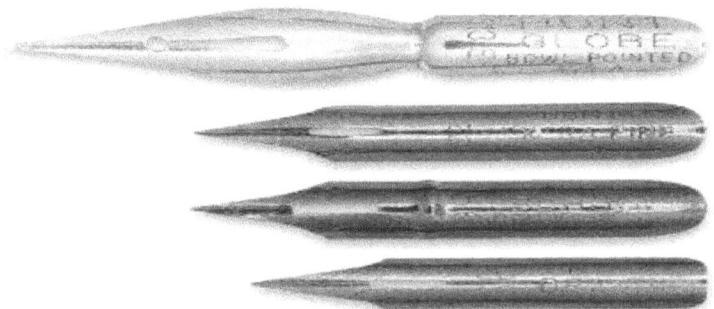

The fountain pen was patented in 1884. They were invented to create a continuous supply of ink without constantly re-dipping the pen but were unreliable for a time. They grew in popularity in the early 20th century.

The ballpoint pen was invented earlier but not perfected and patented until June 10, 1942, which became National Ballpoint Pen Day. The Reynolds Rocket debuted at Gimbels in New York City for $12.50 (about $150 today). Yet they reported selling 1.5 million pens in the first 5 months.

So, there you have my brief recap of how the written word has changed over the years. At least that is a brief recap of the things I found. I am no historian so bear with me if you find something different.

I believe Beulah's letters to Bud were written with a fountain or ballpoint pen as the darkness of the ink is consistent. Bud's letters to

Beulah in 1945, obviously, were written with a fine-tipped fountain pen as there was a constant flow of ink. It would be interesting to see the reaction of Linda's parents and mine if they could see how writing or transferring thoughts happen today.

Grandma Jenny handwrote the "Sketch of Beulah's life" prior to Linda's birth in 1939 with a pencil (The pencil was first invented in 1795). My mother, as well as Bud, used a steel dip pen, known for the writing which goes from light to dark, after the pen was dipped in ink. Beulah would have used a fountain pen because they had just been perfected and the ink's darkness was consistent. And here I am, writing this little recap not using any of the above.

I sit at a keyboard, with no handheld writing device touching the paper. When I finish, I will select *Print* and I will have a written document with no writing instrument even touching the paper.

Well, who gets the trunk now? Perhaps it could be passed around periodically, so our posterity can all read and feel the love of these two people, who were born 113 years ago, on the frontier and forerunners of our modern day lives. That lifestyle has been so dramatically changed from what our younger family is familiar with.

Eventually, there will be another kind of trunk left for our posterity. In it they may find the love letters that Linda and I wrote while she was teaching school in Anaheim, California. They may be more boring than that of Bud's and Beulah's, since there is not the mystique that seemed to pique our interest.

Bud was not dealt a very easy hand in life but was positive and not a complainer, except for the one time I quoted above. Linda and I have heard from so many common acquaintances what a good man he was. I am happy to think of myself as his son-in-law.

After Bud's passing, of course, many people showed their kindness and thoughtfulness. We counted 95 sympathy cards offering condolences and wishing Beulah, Norman and Linda their heartfelt sorrow. They will also be put back in their safe storage place, along with all the things we found there.

After 1945, Beulah worked at the various places mentioned earlier, including Three Bear Lodge. Eventually she moved back into her little house on West Main in St. Anthony.

While Norman was alive, she spent time with him in New York. She loved that time. He took her places and did things with her that she never dreamed of. They would go to Broadway plays in New York, enjoy concerts and ballets, visit the Empire State Building, and spend the weekends just traveling to new places.

Many winters she spent living in our condo in St. George. Some winters, her niece Norma and husband, Harold, spent time with her. Norma said:

> *"We got along great because we both liked movies, especially the old black and white. We would watch movies, sometimes until 12 or 1 in the morning. But no matter how late we would stay up, the next morning she would be up by 6 AM, and get ready so she could watch Murder She Wrote with Angela Lansbury. She also loved watching Julie Roberts and Sandra Bullock."*

When Beulah could no longer stay in her home, we moved her to the care center in St. Anthony. In February of 2007, while living there, she fell. After a stay in the hospital, we moved her to the Ashton Rehabilitation Nursing Home where she passed away at 94 years of age.

Forgive me for inserting a few final thoughts from the funerals of Norman and Beulah, for I was privileged to speak at both. If you knew Beulah the way most did, you will get a chuckle, and yet as I was writing this a few tears were hard to hold back due to these memories that I am trying to preserve.

At Norman's funeral, I shared a closing phrase I'd heard Beulah, Norman, and Linda use, *"Well, I'll be talkin' to ya."* Beulah would use this phrase each time she ended a phone conversation. But one day she started to end her conversation with 'Well, I'll be talkin' and the person on the other end must have interrupted her. She never got to finish, just, "*Well, I'll be talkin . . .*" I couldn't help but chuckle a little bit, because I am sure she will.

At Beulah's funeral, I added more to those words. Now, 17 years later, Beulah has kept talking. She had a zesty uplifting personality. But the last few months of her life, when her speech was slow and deliberate, I never heard her say, 'I'll be talkin' to ya' any more. The Beulah we have always known was not the same in the last 3 months of her life. Her spirit was still strong, but her body became frail and her thoughts and speech slow. She did not seem to be in any pain, and on her last day, she slipped away into a peaceful sleep. What a blessing and a sweet way to leave her little 85 lb. body.

Skipping through some of the rest of Beulah's tribute there remains a theme. I don't know if is doctrinal, but I can imagine that by now there is a whole lot of talkin' going on with Norman, a whole lot of talkin' goin' on with her brothers about politics (that won't be an issue anymore, so they'll have to find a new topic), a whole lot of talkin' with our grandmas, with Rochelle, and even with her little great granddaughter, London. But especially there has been a whole lot of talking' goin' on with her beloved, handsome, cowboy husband, Bud, who left her side 51 years before.

Perhaps it is not the same as the actual talking indicated above, but for the last year, Linda has felt as though Beulah was here in the house with her. She has never had any conversations with her but just sort of matter of fact "Mother is here" feelings. She has related that to me many times. This started to happen even before we opened the trunk and has also continued since.

There are still many more things she would like to know about her dad. She has told me so many times, "you can't imagine what it means to me to see all this stuff I have never seen before. It makes me so happy inside. It's like finding more about the most important people in my life, that I didn't know."

Well, our two families, whose lives ran parallel for over 116 years, were finally joined together with Linda's and my marriage. It is also interesting to note that in Beulah's funeral talk, I said, "You see, she was gone from her real home for a short 94 years, just in the twinkling of an eye, in the eternal scheme of things." It is somewhat ironic that when rereading Beulah's funeral talk, I came across that phrase, which I had also titled Linda's biography.

For her 90th birthday, we asked her what she wanted. She said, "I would just like to have everybody together." So, we obliged her by having her party in our condo conference room in Salt Lake, where this photo was taken. For that occasion, I wrote and read the following:

Beulah's 90th birthday party with family

Grandma Beulah

Birthday November 6, 1912

Ninety Years old is reached just once in a lifetime,
For this special occasion, perhaps I can make a rhyme.
You said, "for my birthday I have just one request,"
To have my whole family together, would
simply be the best.
Of some special lifelong events let us reflect,
As the family around you, we did help to erect.
You and Bud lived in a house by Henry's Lake,
Of it a little sketch Doug did make.
It was into this world that you and Bud, (who most of us
never knew),
Brought a girl who loved horses and a boy that drew.
These two kids were such a delight
And would stay up talking way into the night.
It is because of this union that we are all
gathered here today,
To pay homage to our grandma with hair that
has turned gray.
Now some have gone on ahead to bid you
and each of us hello,
Bud, Norman and finally our Rochelle, and we are all left
here below.
Twas O'dark:30 in the morning when
I arrived at your door,
To pick up your daughter and her satin
wedding dress that she wore.
We were wed in the Temple by the Falls,
And most gathered here today, were once like little dolls.
Rochelle, Stephanie, Mike, Brook and Doug came from
this union,

And all have gathered here today for your
birthday family reunion.
Even our Rochelle, who we cannot see
But whose spirit is here plain as can be.
To Three Bear Lodge in West Yellowstone we moved,
You came along to help; your love was tested and proved.
You helped the business become a success,
And the grandkids you often had to dress.
Several summers were spent in the museum
piece railroad car,
And your love for the grandkids was never
surpassed by far.
Then it was your little summerhouse in St. Anthony
and winter house in St. George,
And we are all gathered here today, on this feast to gorge.
The grandkid's spouses so far are Kevin and Merrick,
Michelle and Natalie,
The great grandkids are Shelby, Kelsey, Drake, Parker,
Erik and Ben and others we are sure to see.
So here's to you Grand and Great Grandmother dear,
To honor you we are all gathered together here.
Into each life there are special people to
hold onto like a rod,
You are one of those precious few that have been sent to
us from God.
With this little rhyme will come a family portrait,
In your most special place, we hope it will rate.
This special day we hoped you would not dread,
It will only be surpassed by the one when
you reach one hundred.
"Families are forever", the prophets say,
Thank you, Grandma, for this near perfect day.

TWINKLE 4

Linda's Brother, Norman

Norman Foster Fischer, Linda's only sibling and last to carry the Fischer name, was born August 23, 1936, at the home of his maternal grandparents, Grandpa and Grandma Young, in Twin Groves, Idaho. Norman passed away March 12, 1990, at 8:50 a.m., while riding the train to work in Bronxville, N.Y. He was 54 years old when died.

Linda and Norman had a good relationship. Linda liked to be outside helping her dad feed the horses and do chores while Norman liked to help his mother do the cooking and wash the dishes. Even though they had typical sibling spats, Norman was even tempered and a pleasant person to be around. He was good in school and liked to read, draw, and do artsy things. Grandma Young liked him to visit in her old age. She would talk to him while he was reading a book, and he would occasionally say, "What was that?" and go on reading. He had no interest in becoming a farmer. Roguing potatoes with Linda, for their dad, was far from his favorite thing to do. He was just not cut out of the same piece of cloth, as you will understand later.

After graduating from North Fremont High School in Ashton, Norman went to the Salt Lake Business School and then moved to New York to find a job. He began working in New York where he became enamored with opera, theater, art and made many friends in that circle.

Linda's Brother, Norman

He dabbled in art and was pretty good with his paintings, one was of his mother. He would visit periodically, and his nieces and nephews were fascinated with the stories, and the uncle that was so different from West Yellowstone.

Beulah regularly visited Norman for a month at a time. When we visited Norman in New York, he took us to the opera, which he loved, and to Broadway plays. Once, Linda and I were invited to his friend's place for dinner. I was not cut from that piece of cloth and in that New York apartment, at their fancy dinner table, I was like a fish out of water.

As mentioned earlier, religion was not to be the cause of family disagreements, so even though Beulah belonged to the Church of Jesus Christ of Latter-Day Saints, Bud did not think his kids should join any church until they were old enough to make up their own mind. Norman was influenced greatly by Don McPherson and was baptized by him June 4, 1955, at 19 years old, just a few months before his dad died. He became an Elder while living in New York. Years later, he told Linda he was sometimes chided by friends who referred to him as "Norman the Mormon." He also shared with Linda that even though he was not very active, he still believed in it and never hid that he was a member.

Norman later moved to Chicago and was living there when a near tragedy struck. He was walking past Northwestern Hospital on his way to work when he started feeling faint. He walked into the ER, past others to the main desk, and said, "I'm really sick and need to see a doctor." They took one look at him and rushed him in. It was then that Linda received a call from that hospital telling her that Norman had had a heart attack and they didn't know if he was going to make it.

Even though Bud had died at age 45 with a heart attack, we were not thinking that would happen to Norman. He was just 44 years old. Beulah, Linda and I caught the last plane out of West Yellowstone for the season. It was a long flight for us, not knowing if he would still be alive when we arrived. We finally made it to the hospital. The doctors told us he had survived, but was still very sick.

I was asked to give Norman a priesthood blessing, a practice that is common for those who are ill. While giving it, I had a calm sensation deep inside that he was going to be alright. I told that to Beulah and Linda and felt that he was going to be okay and that I could go home. I stayed a few more days and they went on to stay with him until he recovered sufficiently.

Norman eventually moved back to New York, where friends and job opportunities called. Norman became rather proficient as a clothing designer. Apparently, this ability was in his DNA, and he was meant to be in the fashion industry. He cut out the cloth and sewed it together for his sister's beautiful dress that she wore at our wedding.

Beautiful wedding dress made by her brother, Norman

We received another phone call March 12, 1990, ten years after his heart attack in Chicago. This time we were told Norman was riding the train to work and had another heart attack. This time it was fatal. He was 54 years old.

Norman at the prime of his life

Norman was the last of the Fischer bloodline. His funeral was held in St. Anthony, Idaho and he is buried next to his father and mother in the Riverview Cemetery in St. Anthony.

Though this may be a little redundant, the following, written by Norma Goulding Stoddard, a cousin of Linda's and niece of Beulah, will add a different perspective on the life of Linda's brother. She wrote it as a life sketch for Beulah when she stayed in the winters with Beulah in St. George.

Like Linda, Norman spent much of his youth around the Island Park, St. Anthony and Ashton area. Norma's earliest recollection of her cousin Norman was playing dress-up with him and Linda in the top of Grandpa's barn. Then they sat on the hay in front of the big open window high up in the barn and Norman would read to them. Linda still remembers this as well. (In my estimation those two traits stuck with Norman. He went on in life to become a dress and clothing designer and was an avid reader.)

Norman attended school in Ashton through the 5th Grade. The family then moved to Nyssa, Oregon, so Bud could work for Uncle

Clarence and Aunt Birdie. Both Linda and Norman became close with their cousin, Viva Marie and their aunt and uncle.

After the year in Nyssa, Beulah and Bud once again returned to Ashton. Norman continued to attend school there until his graduation.

Just prior to Norman's graduation, North Fremont High School installed an illuminated N.F. sign on their building. Norman would chuckle and declare that it was wonderful to have his name in lights for graduation.

Norman had a terrific sense of humor, sometimes to Linda's dismay, and sometimes at her expense. Norman could see humor in nearly every situation and his infectious laugh made everyone around him smile. We sometimes took ourselves too seriously and he had a way of always putting things into proper perspective, usually with a chuckle.

As a matter of fact, I'm sure Norman would have some choice comment for me and Beulah now. He couldn't pass up an opportunity to get a laugh from our "fallen" states as the ice and roller Derby Queens of the family.

Norman developed a great love for reading during his high school years. I remember how he was always reading passages to me and Linda from his current novel. He seemed to have an almost ravenous appetite to read, a love he never lost through his lifetime.

After graduation, Norman attended the LDS Business College in Salt Lake City, UT. It was in January of that year that Bud died unexpectedly of a heart attack at the age of 45. This was a devastating blow to our whole family. I remember Grandma Young saying how unfair it was that he should be taken from his family when they needed him so. She just kept saying, *"Why couldn't God have taken me instead." "I'm so lonely without Daddy?"* Despite Uncle Bud's death, Norman stayed in school and completed his year. At this time, the self-reliant Norman began to emerge.

With courage and determination, I still don't understand, Norman left for New York City. He went alone, with very few dollars in his pocket and knew not one soul there.

As only Norman could do, within six weeks, he had an apartment, a clerical job and was going to night school at the TrapHagen School of design.

This was the start of his career in the clothing industry (or as Norman called it "the rag industry.")

Norman learned to drape clothes and he also learned the technique of pattern making. He was eager to learn every phase of the industry and had the opportunity to work with several well-known designers. Among them was John Kloss, a well-known designer of women's fashions and Arnold Scassi, who recently designed the inaugural gown for our first lady, Barbara Bush.

Norman loved New York and the life it offered. During his stay, he gained a great love and appreciation for art and music. He had had no formal training at this time, but he learned his appreciation firsthand through the influence of his friends in the profession. He read and studied a great deal about the masters and, for the past ten years, developed his own talents by taking formal art classes.

Norman loved classical music and enjoyed the opportunities he was given to increase his appreciation of it. He stayed in New York for 12 years and made many lifelong friends while there.

He then moved to California where he continued work in the clothing industry in the San Francisco/Los Angeles areas. Aunt Faunt lived in Los Angeles at the time and he grew very close to her. Her health wasn't very good, and Norman tried to check in on her every day at least once and usually twice.

We visited Aunt Faunt during this time, and she loved Norman's visits. He always seemed to keep her cheered up. She expressed to us often how she loved and appreciated him for looking in on her and how cheerful he always was.

When Aunt Blanche came to stay with Aunt Faunt, he continued his visits, helped them with their quilts, and they enjoyed each other twice as much.

This was the first time my children really became acquainted with Norman. They always remembered how funny he was and how he made them laugh. How he seemed to know the special places to take us. Even now they'll say "Norman, is he the one that lived in California by Aunt Faunt? He's cool!"

About 10 years ago, Norman moved to Chicago. It was during the seven years he lived there that he suffered his first heart attack at age 45, the same age Uncle Bud was, when he was fatally stricken.

Miraculously, Norman was in the right place at the right time and received the medical care he needed, and his health returned. Norman once again had the opportunity to move to New York, there he was employed by New Hampton, Inc. Clothing and Catalog, as a clothing specifier.

Beulah has been able to visit him often these past few years. Norman loved to share his world with her. They've traveled from Chicago to New England and from New York to New Orleans. She's visited more art museums than she ever knew existed because Norman couldn't pass up the opportunity to spend time in a new museum. Through the years, Norman has always been caring and kind to his mother. Linda said, "He was never a burden on Mother, especially after Dad passed away. He was always self-sufficient and independent."

Through my eyes, I always saw Norman as one of the most courageous people I knew. He tackled life with a strength I never understood, but always admired. He was, who he was, unpretentious, fun-loving and dedicated to living his life in the style of his choosing. He was honest and he was kind and he never changed. I was always comfortable to have him in my world. We shared recipes, talked about diets, politics, art, sewing. The list was endless, and the time was always too short. If I could ask him tomorrow to climb up in Grandpa's barn and play dress up or read to me, I know Norman would laugh and climb up there with me. He was at home wherever he was, whether it be at a concert in a tux or in sandals and ragged slouch pants.

Norman was proud of his heritage and grateful for the family life he enjoyed as a child. Linda said he mentioned many times how grateful he was that he'd grown up in a small Idaho town in a normal family setting. He loved his family very much and drew great strength from his background when the times got tough, and sometimes they were very tough, I'm sure.

One of his greatest friends was his only sister, Linda. He was so proud of her, and rightfully so. Norman loved and appreciated her husband, Clyde for the good husband and father he is and for the kind and considerate son-in-law he is to Aunt Beulah. He was so very proud of their family and what they represented.

Norman was granted nearly ten years of quality life from the time of his first heart attack. It was not without a price, but Norman paid it well. He dedicated himself to the physical requirements of his body, a commitment to be admired.

His death occurred suddenly and unexpectedly–but mercifully as he rode the morning commuter train to work. He was not required to linger and not expected to suffer. What greater gift than that?

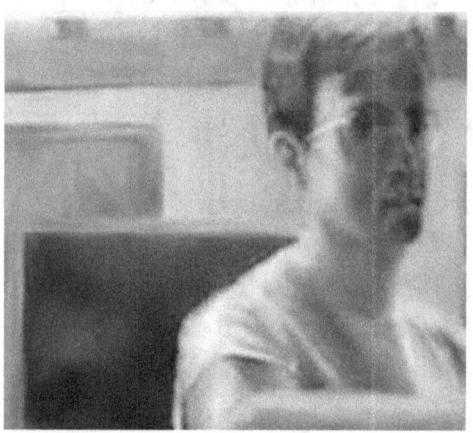

Norman's self portrait

Norman loved to paint. In final tribute to Norman's memory, his employer established a memorial scholarship fund. The memorial, in Norman's name, is at the Garrison Art Center in Garrison, New York. This Memorial Fund will be used to give financial aid to high school graduates who are themselves aspiring young artists with a dream. And Norman's commitment to life will continue through this legacy.

TWINKLE 5

Linda's Youth in Ashton, Idaho

It appears that there are certain pillars of strength that we rely on in our youth such as family, church, friends and school. Each of those has been of pivotal importance to Linda as she grew up.

Linda's family moved from the Railroad Ranch to several different places in Ashton and eventually lived in this little gray house next to the highway, where her dad died, that still stands vacant today.

Fischer's house where Bud died

Linda had friends in Ashton that she often talks about. Things were much more relaxed then and Linda and her friend Trena Egbert would walk along the highway about a mile each way to play at the Egbert's house. There were many who were great influences on Linda's early life. Most Sundays, the Egberts would pick her up and bring her to church with their daughter, Trena.

Don and Nelda McPherson were neighbors and had a little family including a 10-month old boy that Linda would tend. She loved to hold him and squeeze him. Pretty soon when he saw her coming, he would try and get away from her. Brad later worked for us on two different occasions, once when he was about 14 and again at Three Bear after he returned from his mission. Sadly, he passed away at an early age.

Since Linda seldom attended church with her parents, she was influenced greatly by her extended family and friends. She would sometimes come to Twin Groves where her cousins she loved to play with, Sally and Greta, would take her to church. It was there that I first saw this cute, little brown-eyed, brown-haired girl with her big thick braids (a picture of her during this time period is shared on the cover of this book). We saw each other periodically over the years but had no idea that one day we would fall in love and spend 60+ years together and become the parents of five children and 11 grandchildren.

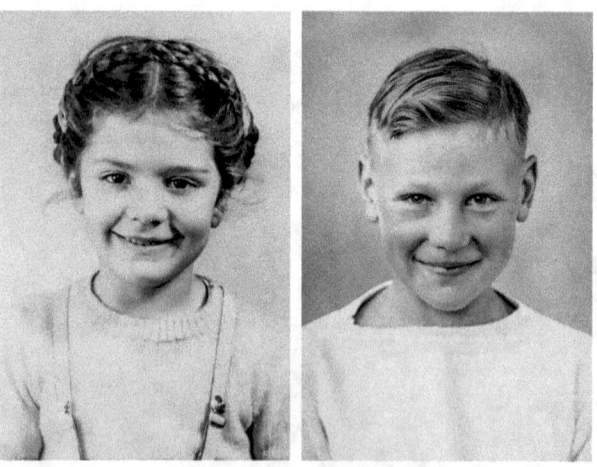

Linda Fischer and Clyde Seely as childhood acquaintances

It was here in Twin Groves, where her dear grandparents, Grandpa and Grandma Young, lived. What once was their house, barn, and apple orchard is now under the highway. When driving over that site it is easy for Linda to conjure up memories of where, in those fun carefree days of her youth, she and her cousins used to play.

Like Norman, Linda wanted to be baptized at eight years old, with the rest of her age group, but her dad wanted her to wait until she was "old enough" to make that decision on her own. So, it was not until she had just turned 17 on Nov. 25, 1956, that she was baptized. Her dad had been gone for 11 months.

The turkey that loved Linda but chased Norman

Periodically, I will use a smattering of things found in Linda's 1956 class assignment paper regarding her life. This was also found in the second "treasure trove," mentioned before. She talks of her friends and how excited she was to go to high school and how embarrassed she was in front of the upperclassmen during the initiation and the garb they were required to wear.

She had her first date her freshman year and was nominated the Harvest Ball Queen. In her junior year she was also nominated Homecoming Queen.

She told of her typical high school years, about the fun she had, and the friends and teachers she liked so much. There were two teachers the girls had crushes on, Mr. Stoddard and Mr. Ritchie, the football coaches. The mothers of the football players and townspeople put on a homecoming dinner in which they gave these two coaches wristwatches. As it turns out Linda has always talked about Mr. Ritchie, this created a common bond with his son, our local Brad Ritchie, married to Bettie.

Linda learned to ski at Bear Gulch, east of Ashton, up the old highway above Warm River. Kids that learned to ski there ended up being good skiers because the hill was so steep. They had ski club parties and would ski under the lights, pause to have something to eat, and then dance in the lodge. I will mention this and the Lion's Head ski fiasco later.

I suppose you could say Linda and her friends dabbled in a preliminary unwanted social media stunt. The night of the freshman dance, they took a tape recorder and strategically placed it over the doorstep where a party was being held. Linda said it was very embarrassing for some of the kids. Today, that seems pretty innocent.

Linda played in the concert band. They won a superior rating which allowed them to participate in the State Festival in Twin Falls, Idaho. She also danced in the three day-all girls dance festival in Salt Lake City. After the event, she stayed with Norman, her brother, who was at school there.

The next day she and Norman rode the bus to Logan and looked around the campus. That is when Linda became an Aggie at heart. She later graduated from Utah State University.

Linda graduated from North Fremont High School in Ashton, Idaho. She was a friendly and attractive girl, but just was not comfortable being put in front of people. She wanted to try out for cheerleader, but didn't want to be in that much limelight. She said that she was afraid of making a mistake and being criticized.

Then she was off to Utah State University, where, in order to help pay her way, she worked as a typist for 25 cents an hour. She loved Logan and Utah State University. All four of Stephanie's kids have graduated or are attending her alma mater. She gave them instructions to send her photos of Old Main and they have continued to do so. They are true Aggies now, because Linda graduated from there they all received free out of state tuition.

Even though Linda is rather modest, I will mention that she was beautiful! She also has a gift of making conversation easy. She dated football stars and others far superior to what I would consider myself to be, a little farm boy from St. Anthony.

Linda graduated from Utah State University with a teaching degree in political science and geography on June 10, 1961. She often told me that Logan is where she wanted to retire. Well, dragging my feet paid off, for even if we could move there now, she doesn't want to leave West Yellowstone.

Linda's graduation day

It was the spring of 1961, and I had just returned from my mission in England. We were cutting potatoes for planting when my sister-in-law, Gail, a friend of Linda's, told me Linda Fischer was back from school and asked, "Why don't you call her up and go on a date with her?" As mentioned, I had known Linda since she was little. She had even dated my friend Darris Bright in high school. Although I had seen them dancing at the summer dances, I had not really spoken to her for years.

Well, I decided to gather up my courage and call her on the phone. She answered.

I said, "This is Clyde Seely."

She said, "Who?"

What a salutation for when you ask someone on your first date!

But undaunted, I persisted and asked her out. Now, 60 years later, in visiting about that call, she related that she was totally shocked and didn't even know that I was back from my mission.

When the designated evening arrived, I walked up and knocked on the door and was feeling rather intimidated. I had not seen her for several years. Then the door opened and there she was, all grown up and beautiful.

Linda, College years

Linda was living with her mother in Ashton. We dated for the summer, which slipped by all too quickly. She had signed a teaching contract in Anaheim, California, and after her graduation from Utah State University, it was soon time for her to leave Ashton and to go teach. Her original intent was to end up staying there along with her good friend Diane (a relationship that has now lasted 60+ years). They had signed contracts to teach for $5200, and with a steady income, they bought their first cars. Diane bought a black and Linda bought a red Volkswagen bug.

Our relationship was progressing to the point, at least, that we would write while she was gone. She invited me down to see her during the Christmas holidays while she stayed at Balboa Island in Newport Beach, California. I was attending Ricks College and some California kids were looking for a ride home. So, we set off, taking turns driving all night in my 1955 Chevrolet station wagon. It turned out to be well worth the effort and paid off in the end.

It was there that we talked about her coming back to St. Anthony to teach the next year. She would live with her aunt Vera and uncle Cy, our family friends. She ended up signing a contract to teach in the same school that I attended in the St. Anthony Jr. High. Her salary was $4,500 per year, payable monthly at $375.00. She accepted a salary cut and a much more common lifestyle, which left me with some great confidence.

TWINKLE 6

The Boy That I Married

(Includes selections from Pebble 8)

The next summer our relationship picked up and it became obvious, to me at least, that we were meant for each other. As we continued dating and got more familiar with each other, her friends and family, who knew me well, turned out to be my greatest advocates. They encouraged her, telling her that I was a nice guy. Her aunt Vera, a good friend of my mother, told her, "Anyone who treats his mother like he does, would make a wonderful husband."

All three of us boys, Dean, Sylvan and I went to England on our missions. After we each toured Europe and would stop in Amsterdam to a particular diamond store who gave discounted prices on diamonds to missionaries. We were able to buy larger diamonds for the same amount as a smaller diamond would be in the United States. So, even though I didn't have a clue who I would give it to, I brought home a diamond and kept it in a safe place until I found the girl of my dreams. That person, one who I wanted to spend eternity with, turned out to be Linda Fischer.

Here is Linda's version of my proposal:

On the evening of August 2, 1962, while sitting in the car out in front of my aunt's house, Clyde was playing with my ring. He took it off and on, and then I felt that the ring he had put on my finger was not the one he had taken off. To my great surprise, when I looked at it, there was a beautiful solitaire diamond on my finger. I was ecstatic. The biggest decision of our lives had just been made. I never had a bolt of lightning strike, but we had written to each other for nine months, we had dated six months, and the more we were together the more I knew this was right.

It was our intent, after we were married, for both of us to continue teaching in the winter. My brothers and I formed Seely Brothers farming operation, where we would farm in the summer. The night of our wedding reception, I was offered a job teaching in Ashton to finish out the year for Mrs. Passy. The pay would be $16.78 per day.

Linda's Uncle Clarence loaned us $5,000 and bought 25 head of Hereford heifers and a Black Angus bull. Of course, heifers are cheaper but much more problematic when calving. Whenever one of them had trouble having their calf, normally on a cold winter night, Linda and I would have to help by pulling the calf with an ingenious apparatus that I had created. Linda was always willing and never complained.

Haircuts were simply just too expensive at $2.00 each. We tried to be rather frugal in those early years of marriage. One day, I had a haircut in Salt Lake and that was the last one I have ever had by a barber. The barber showed me how to comb and crop the hair. Seemed pretty simple, so I showed Linda and since then Clyde's haircuts have become a joint effort. Linda cuts the side and back and I cut the top. Now the advantage with this was three-fold. One, I was able to save time at the barber shop. Two, it was fun just doing it together in the evening. Three, it has saved us approximately $15,300 (averaging out the cost at $15.00 a cut).

Pebble 8: The Girl That I Married

While we were kneeling across the altar, before she was asked if she would take me to be her husband, tears began running down her cheeks. I wondered if she was having second thoughts, or if those tears were due to a spiritual experience that we both were having. I was relieved to know it was the latter. Over time, I've learned that she becomes emotional easily, especially when she is having one of those special experiences that touches her deeply. Our wedding ceremony was all of that and more, as we committed to take each other as husband and wife for time and all eternity.

After the marriage ceremony, we went to Scotty's Drive Inn, got 35-cent hamburgers and started on our honeymoon. (We had our reception when we returned a week later.) We drove to Dillon, Montana, where we spent our first night together.

The bride and groom, Clyde and Linda

Now this may sound really strange to many, but we had previously discussed what would happen on our wedding day. We knew that day would be the first day of the rest of our lives and that we would be setting a pattern. We considered our relationship to be not only physical, but also spiritual and sacred. We had decided to kneel by our bed each night in prayer, a practice that I had become accustomed to on my mission. We thanked the Lord for each other, for our marriage that day, and asked that it be sanctified and prayed for continued guidance. We have continued that practice to this day.

Since our marriage we have always slept close together. One night before drifting off to sleep we were having our pillow talk about our kids, our relationship, etc. While I was just drifting off, I noticed that tears started to fall down Linda's cheek onto mine. I asked, "What's wrong?" She said, "Nothing. I was just thinking how much I love you." That is the kind of love we have for each other. Like our folks before us, we have always been a little reserved about how we express our love in front of others. I suppose many people think of us as all business. But many times, even in public, we slip each other our little secret, subtle signs: a brief touch or a whisper that reminds us of our love for each other.

The summer after our marriage, Linda and I began to work for Mike and Frances Wilson in West Yellowstone at Three Bear Lodge for the season. But what began as temporary shifted into a more permanent plan, and over the course of a couple years we transitioned from farm life and teaching school to this new frontier of making a livelihood for ourselves in West Yellowstone. Little did we know all that was ahead for us.

All of our children, with the exception of Rochelle, were born while living in West Yellowstone. Our oldest, Rochelle, was born May 12, 1965, at the hospital in Pocatello, Idaho, while I was attending Idaho State University.

After Rochelle's birth, we thought it would be nice to have another child fairly soon so that she would have a playmate. However, several months into the next pregnancy, complications set in and Linda began to miscarry. Beulah, my mother-in-law, was working for us in the laundry at Three Bear Lodge and did not know yet that Linda was expecting. (We didn't use the word pregnant much then, it was kind of embarrassing to say.) I ran out and told her first, that Linda was expecting and second, that she was having a miscarriage. She took over the lodge so we could go quickly to the hospital.

I grabbed some towels and rushed Linda to St. Anthony, to the hospital that was 70 miles away. She had lost a lot of blood, so the staff rushed someone to Rexburg to get her blood for a transfusion. It was rather frightening, and I was pretty worried, wondering if everything would be okay. I remember watching her while she was sedated and thinking how beautiful she was and how much I loved her. There she was, looking almost lifeless, having lost the baby and a lot of blood.

Gradually, she opened her eyes and not yet seeing me asked, "Is Clyde all right?" That was typical of her. It was for her they had rushed to Rexburg to get blood. It was she who had just had a jolting miscarriage and whose life I was concerned about.

Yet, the first words out of her mouth were, "Is Clyde all right?" My love and appreciation for her increased that day and has continued to increase since that time so many years ago. How blessed I am to have a companion like that.

Our next daughter, Stephanie, was born March 8, 1969, in the St. Anthony, Idaho Hospital. When Linda was close to delivery, I took her down to her mother's house in St. Anthony with the plan of getting up early the next morning, driving back to West Yellowstone, and opening Three Bear Lodge for the March Snowmobile Races. The motel was not winterized, and I needed to get the heat and the water turned on and ready for our incoming reservations. I got up and was ready to walk out the door about 8:00 a.m. when Linda started to have pains.

Within an hour, I stood at my place at the head of the delivery bed and watched another miracle happen. Everything went normal. Within a few hours our cute little dark-haired, brown-eyed daughter arrived. I hoped for a little girl who would be as beautiful as her mother and I was not disappointed.

In the years that followed, our sons Michael Clyde, Steven Brook, and Douglas Norman joined our family. Like my angel mother, Linda was an angel mother to our children. In the years that followed, our home became a gathering place for our kids and their friends. With the forest as our backyard and the vacant railroad property as our front yard, there was plenty of space for the kids to play. They always had things to do. Plus, inside the house the family room was a natural hangout for the kids with Linda always making these little friends feel welcome. As they grew older, she always kept track of our kids' friends and expressed an interest in what they were doing.

Years later, when the kids' college friends came to visit, Linda always made these new friends feel at home. She would visit with them and had a knack of establishing a relationship that seemed to impact their lives. In later years, when she would see them, instead of just saying, "Hello," she would always ask how they were doing and was genuinely interested in their lives. There are many instances when those friends have told our kids how much they admired Linda and what a great person she is. In 2013, our sons' friend passed away. As Doug and Brook scrolled through their friend's Facebook page, they found a post where this friend had shared the most inspirational people in his life. There were just five listed: his parents, his grandparents on his mother's side, and Linda Seely.

TWINKLE 7

Our Family and Balancing Priorities

(Includes a reprint of Pebble 9)

Linda is very caring and loving. She is kind and thoughtful and affectionately pushes me to be the same. I feel alone and intimidated when she is not there. We fit together as a team; she handles the social affairs while I normally handle the issues at hand and feel more comfortable in those settings. There are certain things that my kids want to talk with me about, but other times, they specifically want to talk to their mother.

Pebble 9 :Our Family and Balancing Priorities

Things which matter most must never be at the mercy of things which matter least.

—Johann Wolfgang von Goethe

After our marriage in 1962, our early life together was really quite simple. I had just graduated with a provisional teaching certificate from Ricks College (now known as Brigham Young University–Idaho), and during the evening of our wedding reception, I was offered the chance to finish out the second half of the school year teaching in Ashton, Idaho for $16.78 per day.

The following year, I taught in Parker, Idaho, under my brother Dean who was the principal. To put the timing in perspective, I was in Parker, standing at the blackboard in front of my class when we heard that President Kennedy had been shot.

After teaching at Parker on a provisional teaching degree for $3,300 per year, we decided it was time for me to finish my four-year teaching degree at Idaho State University. It was here, in Pocatello, Idaho, that we started our family. With the birth of our first daughter, one special pebble was dropped into our pool. Four other special pebbles would soon follow, with each one bringing enormous amounts of joy and life- changing experiences.

As evidence of how fast life has slipped by since our marriage, let me quote from what is now, an old Christmas card that I just recently found. It was a card from me to Linda.

> Dear Mum:
>
> This is our twenty-sixth Christmas together. These have been exciting years as we first spent them selfishly all alone. Later we shared them with our #1 daughter, then #2. Perhaps there should have been #3 but that was not meant to be.
>
> We burst into the boy business 15 years ago this very morning as we plowed through the deep snow for 70 miles. Santa's sleigh would have been more appropriate for our #3. Then we shared these special days together with #4 and then #5. Though we sometimes don't act like we appreciate you for all you do for us, we really do love you for it.

There is no one in the world I would rather spend
eternity with. I don't believe it is possible for one to
love another more than I love you.
Dad

Let me fill in the names of numbers 1–5, those to whom we have
been privileged to become their parents. The names corresponding to
the numbers on that card are as follows: Rochelle was born on May
12, 1965, Stephanie was born on March 8, 1969, Michael Clyde on
December 25, 1973, Steven Brook on March 21, 1975, and Douglas
Norman on May 16, 1977.

Little family in front of Grandma Beulah's house in St. Anthony
Back row: Stephanie, Rochelle and Mike
Front row: Clyde Linda Brook and Doug

As noted, Rochelle was born in Pocatello where we lived
close to a hospital. All the rest of our children were born

in the hospital in St. Anthony, Idaho. But we lived in West Yellowstone, Montana. With the adrenaline flowing, when it was time for Linda to deliver, it was a very fast 74-mile ride south from our home to the hospital.

Each time we learned Linda was expecting, our hearts were full of joy and anticipation as we waited nine months to find out the gender. (Back then there was no such thing as knowing ahead with an ultrasound.) This was only the first of many questions. Through the years, we asked "How will they do in their schooling" followed by "Will they be happy, and ultimately, be successful in building a life of their own?" We shared joys in their accomplishments and empathized with them when their little tears flowed. Overall, the experiences and the emotions of raising five children are legion. I suppose parents never quite feel up to the challenge and responsibility of raising kids of their own. Sometimes we try to spare them the tough things we went through as kids, when many of those tough things are what made us who we are. We think we should have the wisdom of Solomon, when in reality we are just learning too, sometimes with one mistake at a time as we go along. Perhaps a smidgeon of what I mean can be summed up in a few experiences I had with my kids; that of being a doting father over my two girls, and as you will see some unusual rescues and good times with my boys.

Our first daughter, Rochelle, gave us a scare when she was born. The doctor had a hard time getting her to take her first breath. She was later diagnosed with asthma and plagued with it for the rest of her life. Her entire life, we tried to get it under control. Still Rochelle was a vivacious girl with long blonde hair and had a giggle and personality that made others feel good just by being around her. All during high school, she was a cheerleader and a magnet to the boys, which meant I guarded her like a leery father. We had many daddy-daughter talks, and I kept an eye on the clock when she was out at night.

Stephanie was the only brown-haired kid in the family. Often Rochelle would tease Stephanie and say she was adopted because she stood out among the kids. However, her hair color matched Linda's, and like her mother, she was a real knockout, although Stephanie was quite oblivious to that fact. She had a number of close girlfriends that she palled around with much of the time. I was glad for that. We were glad when after hanging out with a want-to-be boyfriend, she would come up and plop down on our bed and tell us all about where they had been, what they had been up to, etc. For some reason, I never felt the urgency for those daddy-daughter talks with Stephanie. Though in retrospect, I wish I would have had them anyway just for bonding purposes. Still, the urgency wasn't there because she was a very good kid, as were all of our kids.

Next in line was Mike, who taught me a valuable lesson. One Sunday morning when I was branch president in our little church, Mike, then about 8 years old said, "Dad I need to talk to you." I told him we would get together right after church, and meanwhile I wondered what was on his mind that he needed to talk to me about.

So after dinner we went back into my office, sat down, and I asked him what he wanted to talk about. He shocked me by saying, "I don't know Dad, you hold the priesthood; you decide." Well, turns out, he wanted to talk to me all right, not about any great problem; he just wanted to talk to me. He wanted to have a meeting with me like I did with other people, so we talked about what he had learned in church that day, and how he was doing in school, and a handful of other things.

My second son, Brook, also taught me a lesson about my time and meetings, of which I certainly held more than a few. When Brook was seven, Linda was bringing the kids back from skiing at Big Sky, and Brook said, "It would be neat to have a dad that could do things with art, like make an elephant like the one Aunt Donna has."

Linda asked, "Do you think that kind of dad would be neater than your dad?"

He looked at her with a cute smile and said, "No. The only thing I don't like about my dad is all those meetings. I hate those meetings he has to go to." Then he added, "Like when he pushes us on the swing, he only pushes us about twice and then he has to go to a meeting." Sometimes we learn great lessons from our kids. Brook's words taught me a lesson and helped me examine my role as a father and, I might add, also as a husband.

Doug was the only one to be born when we were living in our new home. He was our fifth and biggest child, weighing in at 8 lb. 3 oz. He was an unexpected surprise, as we hadn't really planned on another baby. As a result, everybody made a fuss over him, and of course, accused us of spoiling him. Rochelle dubbed the soft little baby roll around his middle "pizza dough." He was always easy to take care of and good natured.

In school, Doug was quiet and unassuming, yet his teachers said that even though he didn't raise his hand at every question, he always knew the answer. We enjoyed him so much, especially as he was the last one to leave the nest. This was a similarity I shared with him, as I too was the baby of my family. During those formative years, I always felt I had a little advantage over my siblings because after they left home, it was just me with my parents. And since I was the last one to live with my folks when they were getting older, I felt a deep responsibility for them.

As I mentioned, Brook's spontaneous, naïve, yet candid, comment about my meetings hit a nerve inside me and caused me pause. The continual tug of war on my time between business, family, church, and community meetings have always been a challenge. To this day, I am not sure if I have always sufficiently balanced my one-on-one time with my kids and other "just" things. But in the end, even though these meetings and other responsibilities took a toll, they also offered a downpour of rewards too.

For instance, I am reminded of one memorable example when I was in the Stake Presidency, a leadership position that covered a large region within my Church. This particular Sunday, I got up at 5:00 a.m., left at 6:00 a.m. to drive the sixty-mile drive to Ashton, and attended my first meeting at 7:00 a.m. After this, I visited two separate congregations and spoke in their meetings. Then I drove the 57 miles home. It was a long and draining day, spiritually and emotionally, and I felt tired and physically exhausted. On top of everything, I had been fasting on this particular Sunday and returned home tired and hungry.

I can still remember and, in fact, feel what happened as I came home to Linda and the kids. Linda was standing in the kitchen. I didn't say anything, just went over to her and gave her a big hug. As I squeezed her tightly, I could feel her strength come into my body. Finally I started to let go and she kept holding on and said, "Wait a minute, I'm not through with you yet." Soon, our three little boys arrived at the scene and aimed to separate our hug. They pushed between our legs and said, "Break it up. Break it up." I chased them all up to our bed, threw them on it, and began to wrestle them. They were all laughing and I was saying, "I'll teach you guys to try and break us up."

Mike started calling out "dogpile, dogpile," and sure enough our little schnauzer dog jumped in the middle of us all, barking like crazy. For some reason, I was no longer tired. And I felt like I could do it all again. There were many rewarding experiences like that.

In the moment of our trials, life can seem a little overwhelming, but sometimes in retrospect those trials turn into some of our fondest memories. For us, whether it was having to get up in the middle of the night and drive my loader to pull out multiple 4×4s driven by my boys and their friends from being stuck in mud bogs, or helping rescue my stranded jeep from nearly tipping over on the side of a mountain, we survived it all.

At such times, rather than lose my cool, I remember when Dad and Mother were gone and my friends and I sloughed school and took the truck to go goose hunting in Island Park. Well, that was the plan anyway. As I was driving around a bend on the highway, I took my eyes off the road. In that split second, the truck left the highway, crashed through a farmer's fence, and stopped only after the front wheels were torn off and left in a ditch. I remember how nervous I was when I tried to explain to my dad why I skipped school and wrecked the truck. I made a meager attempt, and I will never forget

Dad thoughtfully saying, "Well Clyde, if it bent the frame, we will have to buy a new truck." Even though we couldn't afford it, that is what we did. I don't remember that Dad and I ever laughed about my blunder. But my boys, their friends, and I, have had some good laughs due to their teenage escapades that went awry.

With all that I have had to balance, between my family, business, and community responsibilities, perhaps I asked my kids to be mature beyond their years and understanding. Maybe there is a parallel between Dad and me, as a boy, and me, as a dad, with my kids. I never really learned to fish, because the cows needed to be milked, the water had to be turned, the hay had to be baled and hauled, and so much more.

Our kids quite often comment on how hard they worked when they were little. We started them off by sweeping under the mats in front of each of the motel doors. Then they stripped and replaced linens in the rooms. Eventually, they graduated to bussing tables in the restaurant and from there to waiting tables. The boys also became snowmobile gassers (and would ride them around enough to make sure they could do some cool tricks on the way to the pumps).

But with all this hard work, there also came some rewards. In 1979, when Stephanie was just 10 years old, we took her and Rochelle to Spain to see Linda's cousin Russell, and to Switzerland and Germany to see my cousin Connie. My daughters didn't handle the European food very well, but once they saw a McDonalds in Zurich all was well. To this day, Stephanie still remembers that trip and the fun she had bonding with her 2nd cousins in Europe.

Many people from Utah and Idaho buy second homes on Hebgen Lake for their summer retreats. We were fortunate to have this lake in our backyard. I remember with fondness the years we took our boat out, during that magical time in the evening when the water was like glass. The boat cut through the water like a knife, leaving a ripple wake behind. Then we added fifty-foot ropes and pulled a couple of our boys or their friends on a variety of water toys. Their favorites were the bodyboards they brought from Maui. The boys would lay flat on their stomachs, and while going 30 miles per hour with just

2 inches of foam between them and the water, they would laugh and jump over the boat's wake.

But long before our Hebgen Lake memories, we became hooked on what would become our real annual vacation in Maui, Hawaii. It all began when we took our five little stair-step children and bought a timeshare at Maui Hills. We left our long cold winters in the snow to go for two weeks and enjoy the ocean in this tropical paradise by snorkeling, bodyboarding, and whale watching.

But first, the main course of the morning was to build sandcastles. These started out small with little plastic tools but grew as our kids and grandkids grew until we resorted to an irrigation shovel and really got into it, big time. Our prize was a replica of my memory of Chichen Itza. Such creations have grown in size to be about chest high.

When Linda and I were first married and trying to get a start in life, I asked her Uncle Clarence if he would help fund the purchase of some cattle. He consented and then said. "Clyde, you are sitting in the golden chair of opportunity." Now, many years later, our children and grandchildren sit in a similar chair of opportunity. How proud Linda and I are of our kids. All of them have attended college and are searching out their own opportunities to make the most of their lives.

The continual tug of war on my time remains one of my challenges. First with Linda, she has been very considerate of the time spent elsewhere when she deserved to have more time together. I am trying to play catch up there. Linda and I have tried to compress all the family responsibilities, work, church, and community meetings into one lifetime. That is not easy to do but I guess we haven't done too badly. We are proud of all of our kids. They are wonderful people, and as Linda always says, "It's not only what is on the outside, but what is on the inside that really counts."

We have shared some very special times, but among all the memories, the ones I cherish most are the times we could all return to the place we called home to our little safe haven, and enjoy those simple moments that will long be remembered and treasured.

TWINKLE 8

Our Houses That Became Our Homes

(Includes a reprint of Pebble 10)

We have shared some very special times, but among all the memories, the ones I cherish most are the times we could all return to the place we called home to our little safe haven, and enjoy those simple moments that will long be remembered and treasured.

Pebble 10: Our Houses That Became Our Homes

"The most important of the Lord's work you will ever do will be within the walls of your own homes."

—Harold B. Lee

When Linda and I came to live in West Yellowstone we lived in a one-bedroom apartment with a large living room, a warm fireplace, and a front corner window that looked down on Yellowstone Avenue. This was the place where the Wilsons lived when I worked for them my first year, and Linda and I loved the place. Though it was only an apartment, it became a home to us.

Living on site at the lodge, it was convenient to run upstairs to get a sandwich for lunch. But it seemed like it never failed; when I would go upstairs to eat dinner, the bell in the lobby would ding so I would have to run back downstairs (two at a time) to rent a room or help a guest. Linda and I joked that on slow nights, in order to get a customer, all we had to do was go upstairs and eat.

We got along fine in our small apartment until the children started coming along, and then the one bedroom was not sufficient. In time, we used an adjoining motel room as our bedroom and then built on an extra bedroom. We brought Rochelle, Stephanie, and Mike home to that small apartment. But eventually even the additional space was not enough for our growing family.

On June 13, 1978, after 10 years in our first home, we bought some property from Mike Wilson to build our new home. It was on the edge of town, about three blocks from the lodge, right next to the railroad car. In fact, we moved into the railroad car while our new house was being built next door.

It was fun living in the railroad car. Other than Mike and Frances Wilson, who had also lived in the railroad car, very few people knew how elaborate it was on the inside. Linda and I had our bed in the observation room and all the kids had staterooms of their own. There was a large living room with mostly glass walls and the forest was our backyard. It was wonderful.

Through the construction, I acted as the general contractor and hired the building team. We had some contractor friends, Nash and Mitchell, frame the house and other subcontractors do the electrical and plumbing. Then I reserved the finish work for myself.

Once our home was complete, it quickly became a place for guests. It seemed that there were always young friends over to visit or stay the night. After all, we had the railroad tracks with all the train money (round pieces of metal left from the trains hauling timber) as our front yard and a fort in the forest as our backyard. As our family grew, so did the numbers for dinner. For holidays, our house would swell with as many as fifty-four people.

Most of my life, I have wanted to live in a log house, and after purchasing Parade Rest Guest Ranch 10 miles north of town, we decided it was time to build that dream. I drew out several plans and then made little cardboard mockups so Linda could visualize how it would look. We finally decided on a plan we both liked and Blair Anderson, a master craftsman who built beautiful log homes, had a draftsman draw it up accordingly.

From that point on, the project took three years to complete. During the construction phase, Blair found the biggest logs he could, some 25 inches in diameter, and pre-built the house on his Highway 20 property. After it was built, the logs were marked, loaded onto semis, and restacked in its final location at the west end of the ranch.

Seely log home overlooking Hebgen Lake and incredible views

I selected and laid the tile in the bathrooms. I also utilized local stone from Graying Creek for the fireplace, and I hauled up huge lava rocks from my farm in St. Anthony for supports for the large pillars and landscaping. Then Blair's crew did the finish work and we moved in during summer 2005.

Some of the things we love about this home are the spectacular view of Hebgen Lake and the surrounding hillside from every window in the house. We also had a cupola built above the roof line so we had a 360 degrees' view where we watch the animals that sometimes frequent the grounds.

The children we raised in the West Yellowstone home are now bringing their own kids of similar sizes. Here we have sufficient room for all our grandkids to come and stay with us, and we are building new memories in the log house while still finding ourselves surrounded in the front, back, and side yards by forest lands.

Similar to the house in town, the log house on the ranch has become like a pool where all of us drop our own pebbles—pebbles that have turned this house into a home. This is a place of safety, a refuge from the cares of the world, a place where the little day-by-day memories of childhood and family life are being cherished for years to come. Much of the legacy of the Seelys began within the walls of these three homes, each one on the doorstep of Yellowstone.

TWINKLE 9

The Loss of Our Daughter, Rochelle

(Includes selections from Pebble 11)

Twenty-nine years ago, we lost our daughter Rochelle. She was twenty-nine years old. Speaking from this vantage point is different than the gut-wrenching, emotional reality we walked through during that whole process of losing our oldest daughter. Our entire family has fond memories of her long blonde hair and fun personality.

Rochelle Seely

To this day, there are people and places that conjure up special moments of, "Remember when . . ." We have found that by remembering Rochelle, with all her vivaciousness, causes us to keep her near and helps to preserve her memory. There are so many happy things to remember, eclipsed by that one fateful night in Billings. Her body was there, but the real Rochelle, with her bubbling personality, was not.

Shortly after Rochelle's death, we found comfort in a quote that still hangs on our refrigerator and always will. It simply says, "Never put a question mark, where the Lord puts a period." We often wondered why, but know that this is all part of a greater plan than what we currently can see.

The hole in our hearts will always be there, but time has helped blur the longing. We still ask, however, "What If?" What if she were still here? What would she look like at the age of fifty-eight? Would she and Kevin eventually have kids? And the wondering goes on.

Linda has maintained a close relationship with Kevin, Rochelle's husband. Kevin truly loved Rochelle and we loved him. He has moved on with his life but still keeps in touch.

Pebble 11: The Loss of Our Daughter, Rochelle

Somehow, across each stretching mile, I feel your touch and see your smile. As though your thoughts had found a way to reach me with your voice today.

—Author Unknown

It was on August 20, 1994, that we lost our oldest daughter Rochelle. She was just 29 and died as a result of an acute asthma attack. In memory of Rochelle, I will start with her birth and tell a little about the pebble she dropped in the pool of our lives and the lives of others. Linda and I were living in a little basement apartment in Pocatello, Idaho. I was about to graduate from Idaho State University with my BS degree in education and Linda was taking some graduate classes. Early in the school year, I would drop Linda off at class, while she was still suffering from morning sickness, and we both hoped she would make it through. I can still picture her dressed in a black and white frock as she walked into her school.

I also remember the little kicks and movements when I placed my hand over Linda's stomach as our baby grew. Then, as Linda neared the last stages of pregnancy, she went to see Dr. Wight. He said she was about a week away from labor. However, that night she became uncomfortable and started having repeated pains. Something was obviously happening. We called the doctor for confirmation. He told us to get her admitted into the hospital and he would come when she was ready. A little after midnight, we were in the delivery room. I was standing at the head of the delivery bed and the doctor was at the action end. I had joked with Linda before by saying, "I don't know why we have to pay for a doctor. I've delivered many lambs, and you've even helped me deliver calves. It can't be much different than that!"

Of course, these jokes were all in good humor. For the reality was, this situation was much more serious than delivering farm animals. We were about to have a little baby, a baby we had been blessed to help create and who was coming to us straight from the presence of God.

The doctor told me I could stand at the head of the bed, but if I got woozy and was going to pass out, I was on my own. A mirror was propitiously placed so Linda and I could see what was happening. The nurse held her hand on Linda's stomach and at the right time said, "Push," and Linda obliged.

Yet each push was very painful, and as I held her hands in mine, she pushed her fingernails into the palms of my hands. I suppose this was a clever way for her to make sure I also felt part of the joy of this whole experience. It was not an easy birth. In fact, when the little head was in view, the doctor took a large set of forceps to help pull, which would leave temporary facial marks. But finally our baby was out! I watched the umbilical cord be cut, and then we saw that it was a little girl. In that short moment, we rejoiced while our little baby was on her own, and where she should have begun breathing. In an eerie silence, I waited for the typical cry of the newborn, but nothing happened; there was no breath. The doctor picked her up by the feet and smacked her on the bum. He began rubbing her cheeks hard. It seemed the first breath was far too long in coming. However, the first breath eventually came into her lungs and she began the long-awaited cry. We were so relieved.

Little Rochelle was born about 2:00 a.m. on May 12, 1965. Of course she was the most beautiful baby in the delivery room, little bruised face and all. And although I was beyond delighted, unfortunately, it also was a very short night for me, as I had to be at school in a few hours.

A few weeks later, we returned to Three Bear Lodge for the summer. I had one more year before graduation, but we were going to be short financially, so Mike and Frances helped us out with a loan. We worked the entire summer and then returned to school in the fall. Linda got a job teaching for a school in Blackfoot, and I commuted to Pocatello. For the weekdays, we would drop Rochelle off at the babysitter's home, which worked out very well.

However, during the first eighteen months of Rochelle's life, we noticed she got sick a lot. Then, finally, a doctor determined she had asthma. As she grew older, Rochelle spent a lot of time in the hospital, which caused her to miss a lot of school. One year she was in the hospital four different times. I believe it is her fourth grade picture that shows how thin and weak she looked. Nights were especially bad for her. I remember when we traveled sometimes we put her inside a shower, as the steam would often help. Other times we just drove around with her mother holding her, since that also seemed to help, and eventually Rochelle's wheezing and whimpering would cease.

During her teenage years, when she had an attack, I found two sensitive pressure points by her shoulder blades and would push hard on them with both thumbs. If I could find that particular sweet spot it would sometimes ease the attack. I don't know if the pressure hurt her so bad that it deflected her attention off her breathing problems, or if it actually triggered something inside. All I know is that sometimes it helped her breath easier again.

Then, somewhere along those teenage years, we finally found an asthma specialist who really seemed to know what to do to help. He indicated that he thought Rochelle would be able to live a long life by being cognizant of her medications and physical limitations. Despite all of her asthma problems, Rochelle always maintained a cheerful personality. She was not one to complain, and she managed to stay very active. She was a cheerleader in high school all four years, and the physical exertion quite often caused her to wheeze. In those cases, she grabbed her inhaler, took a quick puff, and got back onto the floor.

When Rochelle became a waitress at Three Bear Restaurant, she had the same asthma problem. During those years, smoking was still allowed in the restaurant, and the smoke was hard on her. When no one was watching, she pulled out her inhaler, took a quick puff, and then returned quickly back to her tasks. At the time of her death, she was the main waitress, and we had hopes of promoting her to the Front End Manager. She would have done an excellent job.

Rochelle laughed easily and always exuded happiness. She was a cute, little, vivacious, fun girl to be around. As she grew older, this proved especially true with the boys. They wanted to be around Rochelle, which caused Linda and me some worry and led me to a fair share of those little father-daughter talks. Fortunately, Rochelle eventually fell in love with her best friend, Kevin Burns, and they later married.

Kevin was on the police force and was an avid hunter. They loved to go hunting together, sometimes scoping out the area before the season began. Since Rochelle could not always exert herself and keep up with Kevin at the same time, she sometimes sat and waited for him in the pickup. She would say, she "sometimes scoped him out while he was scoping out the game area." Rochelle and Kevin were happily married for five years. They had an enviable relationship.

Though we were anxious for them to bring little grandchildren into our home, it was not to be. Rochelle had another condition that did not allow her to have children. This was disappointing to them and to others who wanted to see this union carried on into future generations. In spite of this, she seemed to have settled down into a rather tolerable lifestyle.

Rochelle and Kevin lived in a small log house we purchased from Iris McNabb in 1989. We remodeled the cabin, which also had a large glassed-in living room that bordered the forest. Their life seemed to be picture perfect. Kevin was really good at police work, and Rochelle was fitting into her responsibilities at Three Bear Restaurant.

In the summer of 1994 as we were building the Holiday Inn I remember a moment as clearly as if it were today.

I was looking down through an unfinished third floor window to see the sidewalk below. Reminiscent of the past, it looked like my little daughters were pushing a baby stroller with a little doll in it.

But in reality it was my grown daughters, Rochelle and her younger sister, Stephanie. They were adults now and the little doll was actually Stephanie's baby daughter, our first granddaughter, Shelby. They were both pushing the stroller and giggling as they went along, unaware of who was watching from above. Rochelle was a perfect aunt; she was so happy for Stephanie.

But soon after that priceless moment, our lives would change forever. On the fateful night of August 20, 1994, Rochelle and Kevin were staying with his folks while they attended the Billings Fair. Linda and I had just gone to bed at 11:30 when the phone rang. On the other end of the phone was Kevin's mother, Rose Mary. She told us that Rochelle had just had an acute asthma attack and that the ambulance was taking her to the Billings Hospital. She said it was a really bad attack, and they didn't know if she would make it.

The life of my daughter, which the asthma doctor from our past had indicated would go on for a long time, was now threatened, and we began preparing for the inevitable. We called our friend R. J. from Yellowstone Aviation and asked if we could charter his plane to take us to Billings. Within 20 minutes, we were at the airport and taking off.

In the meantime, we called Kevin. He was sobbing and said, "Clyde, I have lost my best buddy, I have lost my best buddy, I have lost her." Our worst fears were confirmed; Rochelle had not made it.

It was a long, dark flight to Billings. Doug, our sixteen-year-old son, sat in the front seat while Linda and I sat huddled together as we tried to understand what had just happened. All our hopes and aspirations for Rochelle were now gone, just suddenly wiped out.

Kevin's mother met the three of us at the airport. We rushed to the hospital and into the room where Rochelle was lying on a table. The long blond hair and the clothes she wore were all still there, but her happy vivacious spirit was not.

We spent some time alone with her, but the realization that we would never see her happy face again set in. It was obvious that nothing we could do could reverse what had just happened. We left with holes in our hearts and wondered how we could possibly cope with this loss.

We spent time with Kevin, who looked so alone. I have always known that we grieve for the loss of an individual only to the extent we have loved them. The grief we shared in that moment with Kevin was incalculable, as was our love. The remainder of the night was short. Kevin couldn't face going back to where he had lost his Rochelle, so he went with us to check into a motel.

What followed in the next few days was the sharing of the grief we felt, mixed with the necessity for arranging for the mortuary, casket, program, and funeral. It may seem inconsequential at this time to talk about the choice of the funeral program, but you will eventually understand. Gary Bidwell, owner of the St. Anthony funeral home, had just received a new program cover on which there was a picture of a deer among some tall trees. It seemed to be looking right at us. Since Kevin and Rochelle had spent so much time in the wilds watching deer and other animals, it seemed fitting that this should be the cover. Then the rest of the program was arranged, and it came time to place the topical phrase or thought-provoking statement on the back cover.

I had never written a poem before but felt prompted to reserve this space for myself so I could write something about the scope of her life. I sat down at the computer and the thoughts began to rush into my head, coming out in a rhyme that expressed a summation of her life.

To Rochelle

I have been honored over the years to speak at funerals
    galore,
But for some reason this one isn't the same as before.
Because of the person who we honor this day,
I just can't get the words out I wish to say.
So bear with me, my little daughter while I pen a
    tidbit or two
That only feebly expresses my love for you.
Just 29 years ago straight from heaven you came,
To brighten our lives, that would never be the same.
'Twas 3 in the morning when you first arrived,

After a scare and struggle you finally arrived,
With a prayer on our lips and a doctor's shake,
That first precious breath you finally did take.
With blond ponytails and a happy little smile,
You had special friends and would go the extra mile.
Then came your best friend Kevin, you married;
For the rest of your life with him you happily tarried.
While your first breath was so slow coming,
Your last was too quick to leave,
And we who love you are left here to grieve.
You would have us pick up the pieces and carry on,
And not look back just because you are gone.
We will do our best to follow your happy and positive
    ways,
Until we have our reunion again one of these days.
This last thing you must always remember,
We love you with all our hearts and will forever.

Dad

The day of the funeral came. On the front page of the West
Yellowstone News was a picture of the town flag flying at half-mast,
which I suppose was partly because Kevin was on the police force and
also because the town wanted to honor the one we all loved.

Cover of Rochelle's funeral program

The funeral was a wonderful time of healing, with so many nice things said about Rochelle. Many friends, from near and far, came to pay their respects to her and lend support to our family in this time of loss and sorrow.

Years later, Rochelle's friend Libby shared her own experience with us that mirrored the comfort offered to us. After listening to Libby, and while I was stuck in a melancholy mood, I wrote a piece titled "Dear Deer" that recaptured the details, the service, and the events that all seemed to carry a special message for us.

August 2001

DEAR DEER

Seven years have come and gone since you left us. Days turned into weeks and weeks have turned into years.

How many times have we thought of you? How many times have others told us they had been thinking of you?

How many times have others told us how they miss you and what an influence for good you were in their lives?

Too many times to tell. Too many times to record . . . On the day of the funeral, it was said that the church had the largest crowd ever assembled in attendance.

The service was beautiful. Many attended the graveside service as the grave was dedicated. While we were waiting for that part to begin, I looked across the pole fence. Standing there, as though he had appeared from nowhere, was a young buck deer. Those of us who had the funeral program in our hands looked at the picture on the front, then at the deer, and back again. Ironic, we all thought.

The deer watched us, walked around slowly, and nibbled on a blade of grass or two. Then he did what I had never seen a young buck deer do: he sat down on his rump with his front legs still fully extended.

Eventually, he stood up again. We proceeded with dedicating the grave and the attention of the crowd was diverted to that sanctifying process. When we looked again, the deer was gone. No one saw him come. No one saw him go.

Kevin said as he watched the deer at the cemetery, he had a strange feeling that the deer was there as a sign and Rochelle's way of saying, "I'm all right Kev. I'm all right."

Soon after, when purchasing the headstone, we decided that a deer should become etched on her headstone.

Years have passed by, and the deer once again returns to the forefront, back into our remembrance. A childhood friend of Rochelle's, Libby Baier, came to visit. She had been gone since high school. This was the first time she had seen us since Rochelle's passing, and she was not aware of the above incident with the deer. Her story was told to us for the first time as follows:

Libby came back into town the day after Rochelle's funeral. She was unaware of Rochelle's passing, and her dad, Harold, told her she better sit down. He then handed her the copy of the funeral program. Rochelle's death hit Libby extremely hard, and she ran out of the house and cried for a long time. The next morning, she was driving out to the cemetery and noticed a deer running alongside the car in the trees. She was driving slowly, and the deer followed along for what seemed to be a long time. When she arrived at the cemetery, another deer was standing there. Later as she was riding the bus to Billings, she kept seeing deer at different locations.

Now, Libby is a Native American and told Linda of her people's belief that sometimes animals can represent a comfort coming from those who have departed. At least to her it seemed to be so. Libby told us of many heartwarming memories of Rochelle, but some are too close and precious to tell here.

It is not for us to always know or begin to understand the various ways in which comfort can come to those who are left to grieve. While there is nothing to say for certain that the deer involved was anything but a coincidence, we are certain of one thing, that Kevin, Libby, and the Seely family as a whole have been awed and have found comfort as we have looked at Rochelle's headstone with the deer embossed on it. We remember the happenings of those days that were so close to her passing. "God moves in a mysterious way, His wonders to perform." Our thanks go out to that dear deer that has added peace and comfort to the lives of those who have been touched by Rochelle.

Her Dad, Clyde Seely

Many letters and cards of sympathy gave us support during those difficult times and helped us know of others' concern for us.

A few days after Rochelle's funeral, Gordon B. Hinckley, President of The Church of Jesus Christ of Latter- day Saints, was visiting Ricks College. Knowing that President Hinckley wanted to go through Yellowstone on his way back to Salt Lake, President Bennion of Ricks College told President Hinckley of our daughter's death.

That night, President Hinckley stayed at Three Bear Lodge. The following morning, while he ate breakfast with his wife and assistant, Linda and I introduced ourselves. He said, "I understand you have just lost a daughter," and then he expressed his sympathy.

We visited briefly and expressed our appreciation for his life of service. On the way out, we instructed the hostess to buy their breakfasts. A few days later, we received a handwritten letter on the personal stationary of Gordon B. Hinckley.

The letter was dated September 2, 1994, addressed to

Mr. and Mrs. Clyde Seely.

I will not quote the letter but he thanked us for our kindness and then wrote: Thank you for all you did for us. Our hearts reach out to you in sympathy over the loss of your beloved daughter. We pray that the Lord will assuage your grief and bring comfort to your aching hearts.

Sincerely your brother,

Gordon B. Hinckley

Eighteen years later, standing at the podium of the West Yellowstone High School graduation, I asked my tall, beautiful, dark-haired granddaughter Shelby to help in presenting the annual Rochelle Seely Burns Scholarship. This little doll of 18 years ago, who was being pushed in her stroller by her mother and Aunt Rochelle, now stood beside me in her cap and gown. I asked her to read the inscription on the plaque that had been written 17 years before, when we began giving the scholarship in honor of Rochelle. I have always read it, but this special time I thought it appropriate that Rochelle's niece read it; Rochelle would have been so proud. The inscription reads:

Life itself is precious, cherish it.

Life is a gift of God, give of yourself in return.

Life is to be enjoyed, be happy.

Life is to be productive, magnify your talents and make a difference.

May you be successful in all you do and help others along the way.

Clyde and Linda Seely

Losing a child is an experience that parents hope will never happen to them. But, no matter how much love there is, no matter how careful and protective parents might be, there are times when such happenings are simply left to a higher power. I may not yet be able to see the reasons why, especially through the earthly glasses that I wear, but I believe the time will come when through a different set of glasses, the plan of Deity will be made known to me in its fullness and I will understand how my life fits into God's eternal plan. It is then that I will understand why loved ones of mine were called home to the other side.

At the time of Rochelle's passing, someone gave to Linda and me a little statement: "Never put a question mark where the Lord puts a period." That thought-provoking statement is still attached to our refrigerator door. We have relayed this quote on to others, those who have also had to struggle with the question, "Why?"

For now, for me, it is enough to know that life continues and that we will see her again. The "Why?" can wait. Still, Rochelle's chapter remains a very influential part of our lives. Her pebble, dropped in our pool, will never stop its ripple effect.

TWINKLE 10

"Linda, There's a Bear in Here"

(Includes selections from Pebble 12)

Linda has had several incidents with bears and other strange encounters, all part of the exciting life many would call frontier living. A bear was looking at her through the kitchen door and she ended up chasing it down the driveway with a broom. Also, she has dealt with a moose on the front deck, buffalo under the front deck and even a pack rat–but, to her, a single mouse becomes even larger than a bear.

Pebble 12: Seely's Bear Stories

Faith walks in, Fear walks out; Fear walks in, Faith walks out

—Author Unknown

Before bear-proof dumpsters were installed, bear problems in West Yellowstone were quite common. One night, we awoke to a noise coming from our neighbor's house. We peeked out our bedroom window and there was a large bear standing on his hind legs pushing a discarded refrigerator back and forth. When he had no success there, he resorted to tipping over a garbage can and rummaging through the trash.

However, the most classic Seely bear story was written up in the local paper and an insurance journal. In late August 1986, a huge sow grizzly and her three roly-poly cubs became quite an attraction in West Yellowstone. At night, people would see them foraging for an easy meal of garbage. However, it was decided by the Fish and Game Department that someone would get hurt if the bears were not moved.

A big, round culvert-looking apparatus with a trap door was baited with some meat. Soon after, the mother was caught in this live trap. Next, it was hard to believe, but they also caught all three of the cubs in other live traps. Then, believing the little family was ready for separation prior to "denning up" for the winter, they transported the mother to one part of the park and the three cubs to another part.

About a week later, at 11:30 p.m., Buzz, our collie, and Shultz, our schnauzer, started barking at the door that leads into the garage. I got up and went down, still undressed, to see what the dogs were fussing about. I opened the door and saw a huge bear. It was close enough that I could have reached out and touched it. (Linda loves telling this next part of the story.) Of course, I was a little excited and controlling my vocal chords was the furthest thing from my mind. I half-way called out, **"Linda, ther's a bear in here."** I hadn't heard my voice sound like that since I was a scared, pre-adolescent boy. From the upstairs bedroom, we watched the bear amble across the driveway and disappear.

The next day I had a dental appointment in Bozeman. Linda and I decided to take the boys with us and see a movie. But knowing we wouldn't be home until late, and that our daughter Rochelle would be gone on a date, our second daughter, Stephanie was concerned. She would be working that evening at the restaurant but didn't want to come home alone in case the bear came back. I said, "Oh, Stephanie, that bear is not going to come into the house, don't worry about it. It may come back and try to get back into the garage where it found the dog food. But just close the doors and you'll be alright."

Well, as it turned out, I had misspoken. In spite of my assurance, when Stephanie came home from work around 11:00 p.m., she was still nervous, so she changed her clothes and left. Yet she returned shortly thereafter, a few minutes before we arrived at 11:30 p.m. She pushed the garage door opener and could not believe what she saw. The garage was in shambles. Things were all over the floor and some sheet rock had been torn right off the wall. It looked like . . . well, it looked like a big bear had been trapped in the garage. Stephanie called her big sister, Rochelle, who came over with Kevin, her then boyfriend, and local policeman. Linda, the boys, and I arrived shortly thereafter.

We couldn't figure it out. It was obvious the bear had been in there, but all the doors were closed. So . . . where was the bear? We opened the garage door leading into the house and out ran our two dogs. Neither could bark. They must have barked so much that they'd lost their voice. Then I noticed the door striker was lying on the second stair going to

the basement. I said to Linda, "That bear is in the house." Carefully, I tiptoed down the stairs to the laundry room. It was in shambles. The cactus was knocked out of the window. The clothes, drying on the rack, were all over the floor, but still no bear. The door into the family room was also closed. I cracked the door a little, didn't hear anything, opened it further, and went inside. The TV was on the floor, the drapes torn off the window, the furniture scattered around, and the door leading into the bedrooms and bath was also closed. Now we never closed that door, so I said to Linda, "That bear is in there and I'm not going in."

I retreated, got a flashlight, and carefully went around the perimeter of the house to look into the rooms I had not been in. I fully expected to see the bear caught and caged in one of those bedrooms. I shined my flashlight in Stephanie's bedroom, and even though the bear had made a mess of the room, no bear was now in evidence. I slowly went around the corner of the house to check out Rochelle's bedroom while feeling a little inadequate, hunting a bear with a flashlight. The window was open, the window screen was lying on the grass, but there was no bear.

So I went back into the house to check it out more closely. The bear had gone through the door leading into the hall, where the bedrooms were, and somehow closed it behind her.

Stephanie's bedroom wasn't too bad. Except that the bear had obviously gotten into her powder and powdered its nose, because there were nose marks on the mirror. We all guessed it was probably the first time she had seen herself and wanted a closer look.

There was also a bloody paw print on the bed. Later, we discovered that when the bear was tearing off the sheetrock in the garage, she must have thrown her paw sideways into a nail protruding through the stud, because we found blood on that nail.

Rochelle's bedroom door was also shut. The bear must have been really nervous by then. There was bear scat on the floor, pushed up in front of the door on my new carpet.

I went inside. The room was in shambles. The bed and the nightstand were

thrown across the room and one of the full sliding mirror closet doors was lying on the floor, broken. There was a large dirty bear paw mark on the wall.

The window had been left open a couple inches by Linda's mother, who had slept in the room the night before. Somehow, the bear must have swiped her paw sideways at the window, slid it open, and pushed the screen out. Outside, I found nose prints that had been smudged on the outside of the family room window as though she wanted to get back in.

No one knows how long the bear was in her temporary prison, but we know it was between 11:00 and 11:30 p.m. Linda's mother, Beulah, had been sleeping in that room and fortunately, had decided to go home to St. Anthony one night early, since we were going to be late from Bozeman. She was hard of hearing and would have been asleep by the time the bear came into the room. If she had slept there one more night, I shudder to think what would have happened with a seventy-year-old woman and a bear caught in the same small bedroom. Knowing my mother-in-law, I like to think the bear may have come out the loser.

The window the bear escaped through and the bed
Beulah would have been sleeping in

That last door into the bedroom was the fourth out of six doors the bear closed behind her. After each door was closed, the bear was confined into a yet smaller space.

As mentioned earlier, Kevin, the local policeman, was there, and he called the game warden. The next day a bear trap was placed outside our house. It was thought the bear would come back the third night. It didn't. Instead, ironically, the bear was later trapped at the game warden's house and identified.

It was Bear #50, the mother of the three cubs we had sighted about a week before. Since she had been separated from her cubs in West Yellowstone, she headed straight back to West Yellowstone. She was observed by the Park Service from the air on a dead run.

By the time she had come back to town, and I had almost touched her in my garage, she was nearly chest high, but had lost a lot of weight. After being trapped the second time, she was transported into the Teton National Park. We were told by the Fish and Game Department that she had one more set of cubs and was never seen again. The radio collar must have given out.

Our daughter Rochelle was waitressing at Three Bear Restaurant at the time. Since the bear made her escape through Rochelle's bedroom window, a newspaper did a write-up of the story with the caption "Who's Been Sleeping in My Bed?" It included a picture of Rochelle sitting on her bed with the grizzly paw print on the wall in the background. Another newspaper article referred to Goldilocks and the Three Bear Restaurant. Other newspaper articles also followed. We still have the colored photos of the damage done to the house when we shared that night with an unwelcome visitor.

Since that incident, bear sightings have become rarer. Though everyone likes to see bears, it is better if they are seen in the wild in their own habitat. Ultimately it saves many bears' lives and prevents human casualties. All of which comes back to the reason that the West Yellowstone Solid Waste District collects and transfers our garbage to a landfill 120 miles away

TWINKLE 11

Three Bear Lodge – The Beginning of a Legacy

(Includes a reprint of Pebble 13)

I will provide a little background as a precursor of what will be found in Pebble 13.

Linda was 17 years old, in 1956, when she first came to West Yellowstone to work. She worked for the Whites in the little motel that was just two doors from Three Bear Lodge. Linda stayed in Islay's cabins with Sally and Kaye Daniels. I remember going in there, the next year, and it seemed you could throw a cat through the cracks in the boards.

Linda's mother, Beulah, also helped with saving for Linda's school but with the loss of Linda's dad, she needed to work to support herself as well. The next few summers, Linda worked for her uncle, waiting tables at the Del Rio Inn, near St. Anthony.

You will recall when reading about the letters found in Beulah's trunk, Bud and his family spent time at the Railroad Ranch. It is in this pebble that you will find in more detail about E.H. Harriman's stagecoach ride through Lakeview, a sixty mile stagecoach ride to what became West Yellowstone. He later purchased and named the

Railroad Ranch where Linda later lived, and Bud spent a long lonely winter.

It is also in this pebble where Mike and Frances Wilson are referenced, who had such an impact on Linda's and my life.

Pebble 13: Three Bear Lodge -The Beginning of a Legacy

Don't grumble, don't bluster, don't sleep, don't shirk,
Don't think of your worries, just think of your work.
Then your worries will vanish, the work will be done;
For no man sees his shadow who faces the sun.

—Author Unknown

In 1958, when I was nineteen, I started working as a laundry boy at Three Bear Lodge. I stripped sheets from the beds, helped wash the linens, and hung them on the clotheslines to dry. Then I gathered them back up and ran them through the big mangle.

Frances showed me a lot, and although I knew how to make myself scarce whenever she got on one of her rampages, I soon learned how to please her. In fact, I could tell she liked me since she sometimes referred to me, jokingly of course, as a "rose among the thorns" (the "thorns" were the maids). Sometimes after work, she took the maids and me swimming in the Madison River. We dove off the old bridge, roasted hot dogs, and had a pretty good time.

While working at Three Bear Lodge, I slept in a little back room off of the office and was on call for nighttime emergencies since Mike and Frances had bought an old railroad car to stay in. The railroad car sat at the edge of the forest on a stone foundation. It was quiet and secluded, and they liked to get away from the motel for a restful night's sleep. Before they moved in, I helped get this special place ready for them, but little did they or I know the history of that railroad car, or that someday Linda and I would own it; it would become a prized possession to our family.

I also did a lot of the maintenance. Since Mike was my boss, I watched him closely. I learned from what he did, and then I jumped in and did what he wanted. I never left anything for him to do that I could do myself. Soon, he told me what needed to be done and then left me to do it.

He showed me how to install Formica and resurface the older furniture. Soon the room furnishings had a new look. He showed me how to work with Sheetrock, which I had never even seen before. More and more he was becoming confident in what he had entrusted me with. This became evident when I could walk through the lobby in the afternoon and find him having a nap in a chair.

One day, Mike came back from Idaho Falls with a big roll of carpet, a carpet stretcher, and a box of carpet tools. He said, "Here, I brought you something," and he told me I should re-carpet some of the rooms.

I told him I didn't know how to lay carpet.

He said, "You'll figure it out."

With no more instruction than that, I taught myself how to lay carpet.

I suppose I have laid hundreds of rooms of carpet since that time. Every once in a while he walked through a room I had just done, and I could tell he was pleased. This gave me more confidence to tackle more jobs. I still have and use the box of carpet tools.

Mike was a short, stocky guy with a balding head. He served on the Fall River Electric board of directors, was very active in the Lions Club International, and served as the president of the Chamber of Commerce. He was instrumental in helping obtain the railroad property that runs the entire length of town from east to west. He was a strict businessman with a soft heart. When there was no bank in town, he often cashed people's checks and also made personal loans to people.

On many occasions, I saw Mike retrieve the mail, open it with his pocketknife at the counter, get out the checkbook, and pay the bills. If he owed it, he paid it immediately. I learned a great lesson from him, and also from my dad, in that regard. I have always tried to follow their example. Though he was like my dad in that he was never one to vocally give praise, I could tell that Mike was pleased with what I did, and he cut me some slack when I needed it.

After work one day, I had an opportunity to go back home for the night. I planned to ride the train back up the next morning and arrive in time for work.

It was fun to be home for the night, and the next morning, I also looked forward to the ride back to West Yellowstone. Dad drove me to St. Anthony to catch the train, and we arrived just in time to see it pulling out. We knew the next stop was in Ashton, 14 miles north. So Dad, in our little old 1950 Chevy truck, started after the train. It was quite a race but Dad beat it far enough so I could run inside the depot, get a ticket, and board the Yellowstone Special.

Then the train started off slow and began to wind slowly through the mountain terrain, past Warm River, and through the tunnel in the mountain by Bear Gulch. I kept wondering when the train was going to speed up, above what I thought must be about 20 miles an hour, but it never did. I moved from one side of my car to the other in order to admire the scenery in the early morning sunlight. It was beautiful.

We passed the corrals and loading ramps for livestock at Big Springs. My mind went back to when I was about 16 years old, loading sheep there onto the double-leveled livestock rail car. I re-lived the experience of loading these reluctant participants at about 4:30 in the morning. There is a trick to loading sheep. They have a characteristic of not wanting to lead but to follow. To push them up the long ramp into the car was like trying to push them with a rope. So, I would grab one by the hind leg and drag it backwards up the ramp and then the rest would "follow like sheep." This was the summer we merged our sheep with Cy Young's sheep on the range along the north side of Mount Sawtelle, just north of Henry's Lake in Island Park.

It was later that I learned of the significance of Big Springs concerning the Oregon Short Line Railroad. I learned that E. H. Harriman commissioned a railroad line to be built from St. Anthony to what would later be known as West Yellowstone. The railroad was built as far as Big Springs the first year. Big Springs, headwaters of the Henry's Fork of the Snake River, became the terminus for the summer of 1907. Passengers could ride to Big Springs on the train and then take a stage about 20 miles north to Yellowstone. Up until then, they disembarked at Monida, Montana, and then rode the stagecoach 60 dusty miles to the sightseeing splendor of Yellowstone. The tracks were extended in November 1907 to the place that was later named West Yellowstone. The first passengers arrived in 1908 and this little place at the west entrance of Yellowstone began to invent itself in order to take care of the passengers of the Yellowstone Special and other visitors.

My ride on the Yellowstone Special ended at 8:00 a.m. I was a little late for work at Three Bear Lodge. I stepped off the train at the large impressive depot and hurried across the street to work. The Wilsons didn't even know I was late.

During my first summer working for the Wilsons, I learned much that put me in good stead for my future involvement in Three Bear Lodge. I worked long shifts and was paid $1.25 per hour with no mention of overtime. Toward the end of the season, Mike called me in and said he was going to raise my wage to $2 per hour. I was dumbfounded.

To begin with, I slept in a little cabin out back of the motel. There were no cooking facilities, and so Frances would have me go over to what is now the Dairy Queen and bring sandwiches home for us. It wasn't long before Mike and Frances took me to dinner with them in the restaurant they had just opened in 1955.

I had hardly ever eaten in a restaurant before and was totally amazed. I felt a little embarrassed to order anything very expensive so I would have a hamburger steak or something that didn't cost very much. At that time, it was about $4.95. Soon, they told me to just eat there every night and to just sign the ticket. Mike told me to have whatever I wanted, but I always ate off the low-ticket items. I was pretty much on my own for breakfast and lunch so I would normally eat cold cereal or something like that for breakfast and cook myself a little something for lunch or build a sandwich. This helped me to save more money.

I sent every paycheck home to Sylvan and the only money I kept was enough to buy a Pendleton jacket from Smith & Chandlers General Mercantile. At the end of the summer, the Wilsons asked me back for the next year. I told them that I would like to, but that I was going on a mission for my Church and would be gone for a couple years.

My goals in life were really quite simple. I would go on a mission, graduate from college, teach school, and farm. Hopefully I could get married and raise a family in St. Anthony. This all started to work out perfectly. According to plans, I returned from my mission, graduated from Rick College with a two-year provisional teaching certificate, and married Linda Fischer in 1962.

I even got offered a job the night of our wedding reception. Since a teacher in Ashton had a retinal detachment, the school needed someone to finish out the second half of the year. Life was great—as newlyweds we lived in a little house in St. Anthony, and the following year I taught in Parker, a little community 3 miles west of St. Anthony with Dean, my brother, as the principal. My salary was $3,200 per year.

My two brothers and I continued to farm in the summer and teach school in the winter. We formed Seely Brothers Partnership and began to increase our acreage. To make use of the land, Linda and I decided to ask her Uncle Clarence if he would loan us $5000. I was a little nervous but got up my courage and explained what we wanted to use the money for: to buy some cattle. To my great relief he said a line that has now become famous within our family, "Clyde, you are sitting in the golden chair of opportunity."

He agreed to make the loan and we were grateful. But on the other hand, how could he refuse the husband of his favorite niece?

In my youth, we often took sheep or cattle to sell and attended the auction sale. But it was quite a different experience now bidding against the big boys and spending money I had been entrusted with. Every time I outbid everybody else, and the auctioneer called out, "Sold," I wondered if I had bid too much. However, I kept that up, until I had spent the money I had allocated, and ended up with twenty-five head of Hereford heifers.

Now I knew that calving out heifers was not easy, but I also understood that an Angus bull would cause the calves to have smaller heads and could be born easier. Linda and I ended up buying a Black Angus bull named Domino. It turned out he was a real find. We backed our little 1950 Chevrolet pickup with my homemade stock rack on it into the coral, put halter on Domino, and led him right into the pickup. It was a tricky ride back to the farm, about 45 miles north, because the little pickup really was undersized to haul a big bull and would rock back and forth.

Domino was about as tame as a big black lab dog. We have pictures of our four little nieces and nephews on his back as I led him around. One warm sunny day, he lay down on the grass in front of the old house where the little bum lamb stood. Domino was lying down, and the camera caught my mother sitting on Domino with Dad standing watchfully by. Then I put my stray hand on him and helped Aunt Eva take her turn sitting on him. He continued to amaze people with how tame and gentle he was.

Clyde leading Domino with nieces and nephews

However, when it came time to do his thing, he rose to the occasion. Calving out these first-time mothers was both a difficult and educational experience, as they often had problems. We started to have the veterinarian come to pull some of the calves that couldn't make it on their own. The cost was $30 each time, so I decided, especially after having my lamb pulling experience, that I could pull calves as well. I rigged up a homemade apparatus, hooked a block and tackle to it, and along with Linda's help became quite proficient at this; even when we had to do it in the middle of a cold night.

Then the next summer came, and I took Linda for a Sunday afternoon drive to West Yellowstone, about 70 miles north, and stopped in to see Mike and Frances and to introduce them to my new bride. About a week later, they called on the phone and asked if we would come back and work for them. Money to finish college was still a necessity, so we decided that would be a way to make enough to finish my teaching degree and to graduate from Idaho State University (ISU). The following summer, in 1964, we left the farm and cattle for my brothers to take care of and we began working for the Wilsons.

Linda worked in the office checking in people and writing personal confirmation letters to each person that made a reservation. Frances was very meticulous about this process and wrote letters like these people were her long lost friends. Linda was very nervous when Frances was around, but in reality, she did very well, and Frances was pleased.

After working in maintenance all day, I worked the front desk with Linda at night. We worked long hours seven days a week but never thought of complaining or asking for overtime pay.

One day, like Frances had done for my sisters, she said, "Why don't you take my car and go to Bozeman for the day?"

It was the Fourth of July, and we drove her great big, new, maroon Lincoln Continental to Bozeman for our one and only day off. It was a beautiful drive along the Gallatin River and was the first time either of us had been to Bozeman.

That fall we told Mike and Frances we were short on money to finish school and asked if there was any way they could loan us $600. I suppose that was the first I had thought of, or knew anything about, student loans. Without hesitation they wrote us out a check, and we paid them back the next summer when we returned to manage the motel.

I graduated from Idaho State University in spring 1966 and signed a contract to teach school in West Yellowstone for the 1966–67 school year. The salary was $5,175 a year, more money than I had ever earned. While our plan had been for me to teach school in the winter and farm together with my brothers in the summer as well as taking care of sheep and cattle year round. We were beginning to like the motel business and were being wooed over to the thought of changing direction. It seemed "the golden chair of opportunity" was really going to be found in West Yellowstone rather than on the farm.

So we decided to pursue the motel business in West Yellowstone. We were able to sell the cows and calves, and the little farm we had purchased to pay off the loan and break even. I turned my share of the farming operation over to my brothers with no compensation. This cleared the way for our lives to begin in West Yellowstone, Montana.

At this point, Mike and Frances were not only sleeping in the old railroad car, which was away from the lodge, they also had begun spending more time living there. That gave us a little more freedom, as we lived in their apartment upstairs in the motel. We loved the apartment—its view from the corner windows, and the convenience of the lobby below.

Linda and I now had a plan for me to teach school in West Yellowstone in the winters, and instead of farming in the summer, we would manage the motel for the Wilsons. That worked well, and we didn't have to worry about making ends meet.

In 1966, when we were permanently located in West Yellowstone, and before Mike moved back to California for the winter, he asked if we would like to lease the motel the following summer. We were pleased and surprised with the offer. But were greatly concerned that we would not be able to do things right.

Mike expected a lot, but was always fair, steady, and let me do my job without interference. Frances, on the other hand, was a different matter. She could be very meddlesome and critical, and when she was in one of her moods, nothing was right. With her long Benson and Hedges cigarette in her mouth, her tongue could lash out and show no mercy. Linda was very nervous that Frances would be breathing down our necks constantly.

But in the spring, to our surprise, wise old Mike announced that he was taking Frances to Europe for the summer. That was a stroke of genius! Under these circumstances, I felt sure we could do the job and handle the responsibility.

We didn't see Mike and Frances until that fall, after they had returned from their summer-long trip and stopped in to see how things had gone. Well, the motel was still intact.

Our lease arrangement was that we would pay them $25,000 per year, and that we could keep whatever profit there was above that. We had a good summer and were able to make the lease payment to them.

Our room rates were $12 for one bed, $14 for two, and $16 for four people. We thought that was a lot of money and tried not to increase our rates so people could afford to stay there.

For two years, we continued leasing. I taught during the day in the winter, then Linda, me, and Linda's mother, Beulah, ran the motel in the summer. During the school year, I often taught in the daytime while my weeknights and Saturdays were spent remodeling some of the motel rooms or shoveling snow off the roof. Meanwhile Rochelle, our first little daughter, was a joy to us as she played in the laundry bins while Linda or Beulah did the laundry.

Mike and Frances returned the following summer but still gave us full rein. I think Mike had something to do with that. They stayed during the summers from then on while continuing to live in the railroad car at the edge of the forest about four blocks away.

But during the summer of 1969, Mike decided it was time for them to sell the motel. I heard them talking, and Mike said he was going to list it with Gene Cheatly, the local real estate agent. Frances interceded and asked Mike, "Why not sell it to Clyde and Linda?" She thought a lot of us, and they both knew that with us the motel would be in good hands. Plus, it would also help us get a start in our life. Mike agreed, and so for the balance of the fall and up until the end of the year, we worked out the particulars.

The problem was that we didn't have any money for the down payment. Dealing with that problem required somewhat of a leap of faith on their part, and a big commitment on ours. They didn't want to receive a big down payment and then run the risk of repossession. We didn't want to invest years into something that might not turn out in the end. They had tutored us for several years and knew of our work ethic, and it also became obvious that we had developed a relationship with them that they were grateful for.

To make a long story short, I came home from teaching school at noon on January 2, 1970 to sign the papers to buy the Three Bear Lodge. I then dropped them in the mail and returned to school. At 2:00 p.m. that very day, someone came into my class and told me the motel was on fire. I ran home to see the fire burning. I felt like

I had been hit in the gut. Was this a bad omen? Had we just made a mistake by putting those papers in the mail? For about 24 hours, I felt ill equipped to handle such weighty problems. In Pebble 14, I share the details of the fire and the aftermath that followed. In the end, the purchase served us well and truly has shaped the rest of our lives.

Over the years, we became closer with the Wilsons and deeply appreciated the opportunities they gave us. They continued to come in the summers until it was too much effort, and after that they stayed in California. The last time we saw Mike and Frances was when we made a special trip to Lake San Marcos to see them. We went out to dinner and had an enjoyable time together, yet they were both getting older. Years earlier, we had paid off the seventeen-year contract on the lodge and had also purchased from them five lots on Obsidian Avenue, which abutted the forest. It was on these lots the railroad car sat and we built our first house.

Clyde, Frances, Mike, and Linda – Spring 1987

Mike told us he wanted to give us a Chilkat Indian blanket, a prized possession of his, which he had acquired from an old Indian as a pawn for $50. The fellow never returned, and it hung in the office for years. Mike and Frances knew I appreciated it, so they told us they wanted us to have it. It now hangs in a prominent place in the new Three Bear Lodge lobby for all to enjoy in a 5' × 7' glassed-in frame that I made. Alongside it is a National Geographic article and photos of this now lost art.

We asked Mike and Frances about their history, where they were born, and a little about themselves up until the time we met them. They seemed quite eager to tell us what they could remember, and I wrote down the particulars. We were so grateful for the things they told us that night. Some of those things are now inscribed on the historical diorama on the mezzanine level of the new Three Bear Lodge. The Wilsons had no children and thus were pretty much the last of their families. I do not say this boastfully, but I believe we were the closest people in their lives.

Later that night after dinner, when Mike and I were alone near their outdoor pool, he asked if we would take care of their affairs when they died. They had made all of the funeral arrangements, but he wanted to know if we could see that they were buried in the cemetery at Fir Ridge near West Yellowstone. Of course, I told him that we would be honored to do so, and that we would put them in one of our family plots. It was a tender parting as we left them, knowing we might never see them again. These people who had played such an important role in shaping our lives, had dropped a large pebble in our pool.

Mike soon died. He was found by the pool with a bruise on his forehead. Frances spent her last days suffering from Alzheimer's in a rest home. On separate occasions we received packages in the mail containing their ashes. We purchased a headstone, and they were both buried in our family lot.

TWINKLE 12

Three Bear Lodge, the Purchase, and the Fire

(Includes a reprint of Pebble 14)

Sometimes good friends meet by happenstance, and sometimes these meetings come through doing a good turn for someone else in a time of crisis. Such was the case with Linda and I, as Three Bear caught on fire and brought new friends, we didn't know we had. Frank and Needra Turner, owners of Big Western Pine, came into our lives in just such a way. Anybody could make friends easily with Needra, Frank's wife and that's what Linda did. While Frank came to help during a crisis in my life, Needra and Linda mainly stayed and took care of the motels. Long after their passing, we are still friends with their kids, Paul and Larry.

Even though I am telling the following story, Linda was involved every step of the way.

Pebble 14: Three Bear Lodge, the Purchase, and the Fire

It's not the size of the dog in the fight, it's the size of the fight in the dog.

—Mark Twain

Three Bear Lodge has an interesting history. In 1925, President Calvin Coolidge issued the first land patent to this site. In 1932, the original Three Bear Lodge was built by Wally Bomier. Its rustic wooden cabins were burned in 1941, at which point he rebuilt the new main lodge office. In 1944, Three Bear was purchased by Mike and Frances Wilson for $25,800. Then in the 1950s, the Wilsons converted the lodge into a modern motel. On January 2, 1970, we bought the Three Bear Lodge, and it caught on fire.

Once I heard, I came running home from teaching school to find the back part of the motel and seven rooms on fire. Our little volunteer fire department was there, pumping water onto the flames from the fire hydrant on the railroad property across the street. Everyone worked hard until the fire was finally out.

After the fire department left, I was alone and bewildered, not knowing what to do next. It was going to drop to -20 degrees that night and everybody left except one man whom I hardly knew.

His name was Frank Turner, the owner of the Big Western Pine motel. We shoveled the huge pile of wet laundry to the outside before it froze. Then he said to me, "Well, if we are going to get this rebuilt by the snowmobile races in March, we better get started."

And get started we did. While I resigned from my sixth-grade teaching position, Linda was able to finish out the second semester for me. We had a dear friend, Lois McCray, tend our little daughter Rochelle while Linda taught, and Frank and I worked long hours to get the motel rebuilt.

Frank was another pebble in my pool—as we began to rebuild Three Bear Lodge, he taught me many carpentry skills that a farm boy like me would never have learned otherwise. Our goal was to be open in time for the big March snowmobile races. Even though we were typically closed in mid-winter, we were totally booked for those races. We got all the renovations complete except for the carpet the night before check-in. Fortunately, our visitors were good at adapting—they were happy to stay in a brand-new room with throw rugs instead of carpeting by their beds.

I don't recall discussing a wage with Frank. He just came and worked, and we settled at the end with what we thought was a fair amount for his labor.

Frank and I became fast friends. One fall, we spent twenty-seven days straight (except Sundays) hunting for deer, elk, moose, and anything else that was legal. We worked together with snowmobiles and became partners in other businesses until he retired at age fifty-five and moved to Utah. He has since passed away, and I regret he will not read of my deep respect for him; however, his wife and posterity will be able to. Frank was a rock of a man. He took pride in his strength and never left undone what he said he would do. I am proud to have been a part of this mutual friendship and partnership.

It was fun to be working for ourselves, able to do as much or as little as we wanted. Linda and I worked well together and enjoyed our work relationship. In those days we had very little business after Labor Day. However, this began to change as more senior couples found that fall was the best time for them to travel. Sometimes we would not clean some of the rooms, because we thought we would not need them that night. But I remember more than one night, when we would fill the last clean room, and Linda and I would say to each other that we'd better go clean a few more. Just as we got those cleaned, Beulah would call and say, "I just rented that room, you better clean another one." We would almost hand the key to the guest, as they were coming in and we were walking out the door on our way to clean another room. We made a lot of beds together, and I still enjoy helping Linda make our bed.

One time someone told me that he wished him and his wife could work together like we did, but they just could not. Linda and I were very blessed. Not only did we work well together, we also enjoyed our free time together.

During those first winters, there were many times when we could leave when we wanted. Since Beulah would always be there to watch the kids, Linda and I skied a lot during the week. We would ski Kelly Canyon Teton Village at Jackson Hole and even at Lake Tahoe.

There never was a better grandma. Beulah's life revolved around her kids and grandkids, because she had lost her husband when he was 45 years old. She loved to talk and visit. She was a real people person, traits her daughter picked up naturally. She worked on the front desk at Three Bear Lodge, tended the kids, and eventually moved from one of our cabins to the railroad car for the summer months.

Three Bear Restaurant/Tepee Motel/ Midtown Motel

Three Bear Restaurant was first opened in 1955. Prior to this, Mike Wilson began talking about a restaurant with Roy Dunlock who was a lead chef at the Camelback Inn in Phoenix during the winter. During the summer to get out of the Arizona heat, Roy would work in West Yellowstone at one of the local cafés. Together, Mike and Roy decided to remodel one of the main lodge buildings and convert it into the Three Bear Restaurant. The original Three Bear Restaurant could seat 55 people, but it quickly outgrew its little space and was expanded to hold 75 people.

The restaurant business provides great rewards, but it is also fraught with many challenges, chefs being one of them. Roy, the first chef, was quite a showman and would flip the steaks on the broiler behind a glass so the customers could see the flames jump high as their steak was flipped. However, prior to our buying Three Bear, Roy died at an early age. His protégé, Winnie, took over the reins.

When we bought Three Bear Lodge and Restaurant in 1970, Winnie was the head chef; he was young and a good chef. He and his wife basically ran the restaurant, leaving us time to concentrate on other aspects of the business. The year following our purchase, Winnie came in and visited with us and his wife at noon as he usually did. Without saying goodbye or indicating he would not be back, he walked out the back door across the parking lot, and we never saw him again. All of us, including his wife, expected him back, but he never returned.

Other times, I have had chefs who could not stay sober, or who would do pretty good for a while and then blow it. Since we were a small restaurant at that time we only had one chef, and he was pretty much a one-man show. If the chef didn't show up, we would have to close until we could find a replacement. One morning the chef didn't show up. I went to Bozeman in the morning and found a lady who could help us out. Before we left Bozeman, we stopped at Heeb's Grocery to pick up some things she needed, and she began cooking that night. She stayed on until we could find a permanent replacement. Fortunately for our guests, I have only had to help cook one time.

One time I listed the chef's position with the Utah Job Service. We interviewed several candidates in Salt Lake City. Jim McCabe came in for an interview. He wore cook's pants and a white shirt. I suppose he was about 45 years old. It was obvious that he was very qualified and when I asked him about his personal habits he said, "I am an alcoholic." Now, normally that would have been the end of the interview, but he continued, "You give me a chance, and I will do you a good job." Well, I felt impressed that he would, and since he was open about his problem, it was worth taking a chance.

This was the beginning of a great relationship. I trusted Jim, and he knew it. I discovered that the way he controlled his alcoholism was by working. Jim had his wife with him, which I suppose, also helped.

He would open the Three Bear Restaurant at 6:00 a.m. and leave after he put the prime rib in the oven, before closing after breakfast at 11:00 a.m. He would go to his apartment, rest up, have a nap, and then was back at 4:00 p.m. to open for dinner and closed again at 10:00 p.m. He worked every shift from when we opened in the spring until we closed in the fall. He would do the same thing in the winter season as well.

One time we were in need of a waitress and he said, "Well, I know this old gal that would really do you a good job." So we brought her up. Her name was Kate, and she was a perfectionist. She soon began running the front end and was the trainer for the wait staff. Like Jim, she was older and experienced and had a quick wit and sense of humor. It was not until several years later that we found out that this "old gal" was actually Jim's sister. He didn't want us to give her any special treatment or pressure us into hiring her.

We enjoyed many years with Jim without problems. Then one fall, Linda and I were in New York on a sales trip, and I got a call from one of the local bars in West Yellowstone. Apparently, Jim had come in for a drink. Of course, to an alcoholic, there is no such thing as one drink. There is a Japanese proverb that says, "A man takes a drink, then the drink takes a drink, and then the drink takes the man." Jim had passed out sitting in the corner, so the bartender called the police to take him home.

The next morning, after Jim had a chance to sober up, I called him. I asked what had happened and he said he thought he could go over and have one drink and would be able to handle it.

I said, "You know I am back east and cannot be there in time to help." I explained that I trusted him and depended on him. I asked him, "Jim, I really need your help, can I count on you to pull yourself together and get the restaurant open for dinner tonight?"

He did, and by the time we got back everything was running smoothly.

Jim and Kate were two of many people who influenced my life, as I have influenced theirs. Jim eventually retired and was greatly missed. Several years later, Kate fell in the kitchen and broke her hip.

We kept in touch with them until the end. Jim died first at about age seventy-four, and then Kate passed away in her late '80s.

As I look back now over 40 years of my life in West Yellowstone, there have been many people who have had a great influence on my life, dropped pebbles in our pool so to speak. I owe a debt of gratitude to many more than I can adequately write about in this book.

I have found over the years that learning good business practices is sometimes not as challenging as mastering human relations. If a company does not have a cohesive group of employees that work together harmoniously, customers can feel it.

Because personnel issues continually surface, there are many times, due to my position, that only I am able to address these issues. Probably the most important qualities in dealing with employees are the ability to empathize with them and to be a good listener. Confrontations often occur between employees, and I learned a long time ago that there are always two sides to every story. Sometimes it is tempting to listen to one person's concerns and make a snap decision, only to have to reverse it when the other side is heard. Through my experiences, I have found that if I take the time to sit down and listen to concerns from both sides, a fair decision can be made and the problem resolved.

Some problems require the wisdom of Solomon. I had a manager at one facility who was really a nice guy, but he would listen to one person and make a decision based on what that employee wanted to hear and seemed best for them. Then he would listen to the other person's side and make a decision that this other employee wanted to hear and seemed best for them. He hadn't really solved anything because he had neither resolved the conflict nor made a sustainable decision. I thought back to my dad's statement, "Clyde, sometimes you just have to put your heart in your pocket and do what has to be done." It is sometimes hard to be firm and make a decision that can't please everybody. It is also hard to release employees, but sometimes that also needs to be done. Our employees are all part of a big partnership, and talking through the problem, in such a way as not to lose respect, helps to make us all successful.

With the increasing demand because of the successful winter operation and the need to serve larger groups prime rib dinners, Linda and I along with Bill and Carole, decided to purchase the Tepee Motel and Restaurant and move the Three Bear Restaurant to that location.

The Tepee Inn was among the early twentieth century businesses in West Yellowstone. It was a charming two-story log structure that housed a bar, dance floor, café, and rooms. The Tepee Inn was built by Val Buchanan in 1921 and the building materials cost $1,750. This rather large two-story log structure was prominent for its time. The impressive rock fireplace and backbar, made from rhyolite stone, still stands today as a sentinel of the lively times that used to happen there years ago.

J. H. Venable sold the Tepee to A. K. (Kayle) Clawson in 1952. A fire caused by a burning grease trap burned the Tepee in 1965. The exterior rock wall and interior backbar survived the fire. The building was re-built as a single story structure, and Clawson added the Teepee Motel to the building. We purchased the Tepee from Clawson on May 25, 1978, but we didn't begin our remodeling project and relocating the new Three Bear Restaurant and Grizzly Lounge until summer 1984.

I wanted to build a log structure using local logs and retain the historic rock fireplace. Bill Schaap was my manager at Three Bear Lodge at the time and shared my zest for challenging projects. We got a logging permit near the South Fork of the Madison River and were able to cut and load huge logs with my old loader and haul them to town. We were fortunate to get these big LodgePole Pines, just 5 miles west of town, just before the Forest Service closed this area to logging. It was fun to be able to cut these trees like the old timers in West Yellowstone did and contribute to the rustic charm of West Yellowstone.

Years earlier, I had noticed that on the inside of the Old Faithful Inn, built in 1903, logs were sawed in half to give a full log appearance, So we had David Rightenour, son of Herk Rightenour who had owned a saw mill in town since the 1920s, saw the logs down the middle and stack them on top of each other. Few people knew that they were not full logs. We used every person who could pull a drawknife to peel the bark off all sizes of logs. The big logs were for the exterior and select areas for the interior, while the small logs were for the majority of the interior décor. We still have people like my nephew Tai come and say, "I remember when I helped peel those logs."

We also honored West Yellowstone's past by gathering photos of the early days from the park's archives and from old timers around town. As usual, there was a deadline we were shooting for. We started construction after Labor Day, and our goal was 5.

Converting the Tepee Bar into the new Three Bear Restaurant

In addition to the front Tepee building, there was a 16-unit motel operated from an office and a manager's apartment to the north of the restaurant and lounge. We operated this as a separate motel for several years. On January 1, 1982, we also purchased the Midtown Motel across the alley from the Tepee.

It is always a challenge to keep an old facility upgraded to provide modern and first class accommodations. This has required continual effort on our part. After purchasing the Tepee and remodeling the restaurant, we remodeled the Tepee Motel and the Midtown Motel, both of which were contiguous to the forty-two units of Three Bear Lodge. For economies of scale, we eventually consolidated the three motels into one. This eliminated the need to maintain three offices. The Tepee Motel and Midtown Motel ceased to exist. They both became part of Three Bear Lodge/Motel. Since they were now part of Three Bear, it was necessary that all three properties were equivalent in quality.

On March 15, 1990, we began a four phase, one-and-a-half-year rebuilding project at Three Bear Lodge. We had made a decision to either tear down or strip to the studs the old sections of the Three Bear Lodge that had not been rebuilt after the fire in 1970. We made an announcement in the local paper that a newly upgraded facility would be ready in 1991. We tore down one section, put in a basement to accommodate snowmobile rental clothing and hot tubs, and put in an all-new electrical and water supply system in another section. This gave a face-lift to the entire property by making the Tepee and Midtown rooms larger, upgrading the exterior, and giving all buildings the same look as the rest of the new Three Bear Lodge.

Over the years I have benefited from a drafting class I took my senior year of high school. With almost every project I have undertaken, I have taken out my inexpensive scale ruler and graph paper to scale room sizes, furniture, and design concepts for the exterior and interior. This has helped me to visualize and design the end result I was looking to achieve and to figure out the steps necessary to get there.

TWINKLE 13

Oregon Short Line's Vice Presidential Railcar

(Includes a reprint of Pebble 15)

No one knows how many trips the OSL 1903 made to Yellowstone carrying the Vice President of Union Pacific. When E.C.Manson, Superintendent of Transportation at the railroad retired in 1935, he also retired the OSL 1903 to a place he loved, West Yellowstone.

In 1975 we purchased the property and the OSL1903 on which it sat. Ralph Barger, an expert on old railroad cars, wrote Linda and I a letter stating that *"It is worthy of display at the Smithsonian Institution."* We ended up putting it on display at the Holiday Inn for all to enjoy. It is now 120 years old. Pebble 15 tells the story in much more detail.

Pebble 15: The Oregon Short Line 1903 Railroad Car

No one cares how much you know, until they know how much you care.

—Theodore Roosevelt

In 1975, Linda and I became custodians of a historical treasure, though at the time we didn't understand its full significance. To understand the full story, we need to go back over a century, to 1903 when the Pullman Palace Car Shops in Pennsylvania were commissioned to build a luxury accommodation for the vice president of the Oregon Short Line Railroad. This splendid railroad car, christened the OSL 1903, was built at a cost of $16,850 (equal to hundreds of thousands in today's dollars). We were ignorant of the car's distinguished history until one day in 1992. While we were out of town, a man came looking for our particular railroad car. Gus Tureman, a friend of ours, let him in to look at the car. His name was Ralph Barger, and he had written a book entitled Union Pacific Business Cars 1870–1991. There on page 121 were two pictures of our railroad car.

With this new information, the appointments of the railroad car made more sense to us. There were obviously servant's quarters where the porter and cooks slept which were separated by a door from the VIP section. The executive section was made of beautiful and intricate ribbons of tiny little pieces of inlaid wood (about thirteen per inch), which adorned the Honduran Mahogany walls. There were intricate little decorative railings on top of the cabinets and unique hand sinks that could be pulled down and lifted up so the used water would run out on the tracks below. There were also a couple of little upholstered benches. Under the lids, there was a toilet with a brass handle so one could flush the toilet—you guessed it—onto the track below. One stateroom was made for the ladies out of Birdseye Maple. It was more feminine in design, with a deep red ceiling highlighted with gold brocade and brass colored lamps.

Three of the staterooms had bunks that could be pulled down to accommodate additional guests. One of these classic staterooms had been converted into a tiled bathroom. After we removed the wall tile, we found the big brass key and opened the bunk. There it was, a bunk that looked like it could have been slept in the night before, when in reality it had not been opened for 60 years. It had the original mattress and the gear-and-chain apparatus that lowered the bunk to a horizontal position.

The dining and observation room included a table with leaves so it could be expanded and cabinet drawers lined with a fancy green material to keep the silverware from rattling. Since this was a working vice presidential car, there was also a secretariat in which the secretary could pull down the front to make a desk where a typewriter was undoubtedly kept. This desk had lots of interesting, almost secret, compartments and drawers for important documents.

The OSL 1903 was then retrofitted between 1912 and 1915. At that time, it was renamed "OSL 150." Mr. Barger also stated that it was retired in December 1934 "at West Yellowstone?" The question mark indicating he did not know which state West Yellowstone was in (sometimes that still happens). On June 15, 1993, Mr. Barger wrote us a two-page letter discussing the condition of the car and indicating how happy he was to finally see it. He said that "of all the old railroad cars I have seen in the wild, they're nothing but a pile of rubble compared to this car."

The pictorial evidence backs up the assertion that this was one of the most sumptuously appointed railroad cars in the county at the time. It just so happened that on the page opposite the photos of OSL 1903, there are photographs of E. H. Harriman's private presidential car, built in 1900. The OSL 1903 was obviously nicer, as was attested by some of the employees who had ridden in E. H. Harriman's car and then after riding in the new OSL 1903 remarked, "We out-bested old E. H. on this trip."

The Oregon Short Line 1903, now changed to OSL 150 was given as a retirement gift to Mr. E. C. Manson, a superintendent of the railroad. We found two large envelopes under one of the drawers in the secretary's desk addressed to him. Since he loved Yellowstone, they pulled this vice presidential car up the tracks one last time, built a spur off the railroad tracks, removed the trucks (wheels) and placed the railroad care on a stone foundation. It sat there for 61 years, from 1934 to 1995, on a lot on Obsidian Avenue.

Oregon Short Line 1903. Its historical elegance was once again discovered.

July 3, 1956, Henry Casper, the original druggist in West Yellowstone, purchased the railroad car as summer lodging for his help. In 1958, the summer I came to work at West Yellowstone, he sold the railroad car to Mike and Frances Wilson. The Wilsons also bought several adjoining lots on both sides of this property. (I believe from Ken Chandler of Smith and Chandler's store on Yellowstone Avenue, which is still in existence today.) After Linda and I were married, and came back to work for them, the Wilsons had a large, glassed-in living room built onto the car. With the forest boundary right out their front window, there was a wonderful feeling of quiet and seclusion.

In 1975, when the Wilson's ceased coming to West Yellowstone for the summers, they sold us the railroad car and the six lots that ran along Obsidian Avenue and the forest. It was on the lot and a half, next to the railroad car, that we built our new home.

During the summer we built our house, we lived in the railroad car. Rochelle, Stephanie and Mike each had a posh stateroom for a bedroom. Linda, our baby Brook, and I slept in the large dining and observation room in front. After our house was finished, we let Beulah (Linda's mother) live there. For many years after that, family members or summer helpers resided there.

However, after we realized its historical significance, we were determined to give the wonderful old car the setting it deserved. We would restore it and place it on display for all to see at the new hotel we were going to build, the Holiday Inn.

Yet, it was quite a project to refurbish the OSL 1903. It took us longer to restore the railroad car than it did to build the hotel around it. Jim Keeler from Salt Lake was the chief restorer, and with his guidance we removed and polished over 3,000 pieces of brass, from screws to the rails on the observation platform.

Through the decades, the old car endured severe winters and extreme temperatures which created constant maintenance problems. I had painted it several times on the outside and was constantly patching the roof to prevent leaks (fortunately little water damage ever occurred on the inside paneling). Now in restoration mode, we sanded off many coats of paint in order to get down to the original Pullman green. Then we painted a replica of the original lettering on the sides to replicate the Pullman company photo. It says in Barger's book that the floor plan and elevation drawings had not been found. But when he came to visit the car, there they were, the original blueprint, encased in a decorative, glassed in case. It was standard procedure to place it in this location, just outside the kitchen in the hallway of the servant's quarters. This blueprint was always prominently posted so those planning the train route could make sure the car could fit through the tunnels and openings on the route. Otherwise, if they messed up on this, it would be like a camel trying to go through the "eye of a needle" at 50 miles an hour.

During the time of transition, between being an old relic to becoming a museum quality executive railroad car in its new location, I made every effort to restore the car in its original condition. The original kitchen equipment could not be obtained, so I turned the kitchen area into a diorama displaying photos of old West Yellowstone and of stagecoaches on the recovered window screens and some old window frames, and covered the walls with pleated fabric.

Today it can be visited in a museum-like setting with a photo display of the restoration process. The car's new setting includes a railroad crossing complete with rails, planks, and an antique marble reflector sign on the west end of the car. Hotel guests drive their vehicles across this on the way to the hotel lobby. On its east end, we built a regular railroad track leading into the building so it looks like we just pulled the car right into where it is permanently located. It was here that I drove in our very own golden spike.

Many guests have enjoyed this rare chance to see this museum-quality executive railroad car. It is truly one of a kind.

TWINKLE 14

Property Acquisitions During Our Younger Years

In the winter time, most of the businesses in West Yellowstone had their windows boarded up and closed for the winter. About the only activity was shoveling snow and sitting around playing cards. We never even dreamed of keeping open in the winter.

One of the few lodging facilities that stayed open was the Stagecoach Inn. It was fairly new and had been built in 1948 by Howard Kelsey, who also was involved in the Lion's Head ski hill. He promoted the ski hill to help fill his new hotel. A few other lodging properties were in existence like the Tepee Inn and the Madison Hotel, but most closed down for the winter.

The Lion's Head Ski Hill Is located about eight miles straight west of West Yellowstone. Linda tells in her high school report that the ski club planned a trip to Lion's Head. The advisor could not come so several cars of boys and girls went anyway. They had a great time until it started to blizzard.

As so often happens even today, the wind kept blowing and closed the roads on Henrys Lake Flat (Over the years, things have changed in that area, but the road closure across Henrys Lake Flat is not one of them).

Linda and her friends called their folks to let them know they were snowed out. Panic set in by the parents as to what was going to happen to this mixed group of kids sleeping in the cars all night alone. The kids got in touch with the highway department, and they eventually sent a special snowplow.

In the meantime, the kids had fun talking and dancing in a lodge that no longer exists. When the plow did come, with the blizzard still raging, it took about two hours for the plow, followed by the students' cars, to go across Henrys Lake Flat. They finally made it to Mack's Inn, where they fixed supper and waited till the rest of the roads opened up. Some of the parents got together and defied the odds to drive through the closed roads so their kids could follow them back out.

Well as you can imagine, all turned out well and the kids arrived home safe and unscathed. As mentioned earlier, they also skied at Bear Gulch, another ski hill near Warm River, about 12 miles east of Ashton. The "Bear Cat" was a very steep run and anyone who could ski it became a good skier. Linda managed it, but years later when I tried it with her, it was too much for me.

Lion's Head was less steep and years after it closed, I would take our three sons there to snowboard. The poles for the lifts were still visible, but long since ceased functioning, so I became the lift by taking each boy to the top of the hill on the back of my snowmobile for them to then snowboard down. Back and forth, up and down we went. It was like the boys had their own ski hill and could always ride in fresh powder.

That was our memory of Lion's Head ski hill when our boys were younger. The Lion's Head has since become well known in the snowmobile world as a fun and challenging area.

Why would anybody want to come to West Yellowstone, even if they could get here in the winter? Not everyone skied, and cross country was a laborious feat with 7 ft. long skis and no groomed trails. The tourism season was basically from Memorial Day to Labor Day. There was a sawmill mill that produced studs, where Grizzly Park is now. There were a few stores, with dedicated owners, who would work all summer to get enough money, then spend most of it during the winter, so they could open again the next summer.

The population in 1960 was 500 people. I don't know what the unemployment rate was in the winter. Many folks, like our Mike and Frances Wilson, would spend the winters in California.

For us, our plan was set. In the winter, I would teach and be free to work after school, shoveling roofs or doing some rudimentary remodeling. Linda would be a stay-at-home mom, taking care of our little Rochelle, and, the good Lord willing, more family to follow. During the summertime, Linda was very involved in the business working at the front desk, answering phones, writing personalized letters on the typewriter to each who had called or made a reservation, as well as supervising the housekeepers.

Linda loved the Restaurant. She would fill in as hostess, busser, cashier or whatever position was necessary. She loved Jim, our reformed alcoholic cook and "this old gal I know," Kate, who turned out to be Jim's sister, that he wanted us to hire. Kate was from the "old school," and was in the twilight of her life. She ran the front end of the restaurant with an iron hand, yet people loved her for it. Linda often commented on how Kate gave us a standard to follow.

Everything was going smoothly until we received the biggest challenge of our life. Our whole world changed, as was mentioned in Pebble 14 of my book, when the Lodge caught on fire. I had been told to leave the pilot light burning in the laundry water heater at Three Bear, even though we drained the water heater for the winter. I had just signed the papers to buy Three Bear. I had just put the papers in the mail at noon and went back to teach school. At 2:00 PM someone burst into my room and said the Motel was on fire.

The volunteer fire department did a great job in putting out the fire after only 7 rooms were burned. I had to quit teaching to rebuild, and Linda finished out the rest of the year for me teaching 6th grade. Frank Turner, my newfound friend, said, if we are going to get this rebuilt by the March races, we better get started.

We had an old Johnsons Ski Horse snowmobile that we would ride on weekends and after school. It was fun and exhilarating to ride effortlessly over the snow at a whopping 20 miles an hour. We went into Yellowstone and ate our frozen lunch on the cold steps of the Old Faithful Inn. The roads were not groomed. But we began to envision the whole world being able to see what was in our estimation, the world's best kept winter secret, "Winter in Yellowstone." Then we rode to Two Top Mountain on ungroomed trails with unbelievable snow ghosts, a term used to describe heavily coated trees completely covered with snow or ice.

Needless to say, our plans to close in the winter for me to teach school were shot. Since we were rebuilding the motel, we decided to keep the lodge and restaurant open in the winter. Thus began Linda's and my traveling all over with Western Airlines promoting "Winter in Yellowstone."

While our marketing efforts worked out great, additional property purchase opportunities kept knocking at our door. We opened each door, but not fully until Linda felt good about it. Linda was always my litmus test as to what new opportunities we should pursue. Her hesitation matched what Franklin D. Richards said, "Why should we risk everything we have, for something that we don't need?" Though she didn't know of this quote until lately, that is her through and through.

With a certain purchase, If she couldn't feel good about expanding we didn't. Looking back, her cautious approach served us well. The question became: Is this an opportunity or just another fruitless obligation? As wild as some purchases may have been, I do not recall ever expanding property or projects without her approval.

I am including a listing of the various properties that Linda and I have been involved in developing. Though it may seem it is just my story, Linda has been involved every step of the way. I guess we can be considered 'old timers' now and it may be appropriate to review, for historical purposes, the way some things have changed and have been developed over the years. Many of the newcomers to town will not remember the way things used to be before these changes happened. And in West Yellowstone, there is nothing as constant as change.

A walk down memory lane; property we purchased

For over 50 years, Linda and I have been involved in building, purchasing, and running a number of businesses. Time moves ever onward and tends to leave some things behind and forgotten unless they are recorded in a document such as this to preserve the historical significance.

I will attempt to summarize our acquisition and development of property. West Yellowstone was still in its infancy, and we wanted to not only expand our businesses but to help in the development of West Yellowstone to become a year-round destination town.

I came to work in 1958 as a laundry boy at Three Bear Lodge at the age of eighteen. Linda came the following year and worked at the Tally Ho Motel. After our marriage in 1962, we began working at Three Bear Lodge. The Wilsons took a liking to us and sold us the Lodge on January 2, 1970, when we were just 31 years old. I was more aggressive, and Linda was more cautious about making such a large investment.

As mentioned earlier, she became the litmus test that ultimately gave me the green light, caution light or red light. For all the following purchases and developments, we discussed them together, and once decided, she supported me in every effort. These were also the formative years for our children, where Linda's main responsibility was to be a stay-at-home mom.

As has been mentioned Three Bear caught on fire the very day, I put the papers in the mail to buy it. I have placed headings indicating the other properties we developed over the years.

Morris Motel – Ambassador Motor Inn
(Holiday Inn will follow in Twinkle 15)

Soon after we had completely rebuilt Three Bear Lodge in 1970, the Morris Motel went up for sale. Since Frank Turner and I had become good friends while rebuilding Three Bear, and we both shared the same work ethic, we decided the Morris Motel was an opportunity for us to go into business together.

The motel was a rose-colored, two story, cinder block, 52-unit building named after Ed and Edna Morris. Ed had passed away and Edna was remarried to Gene Adams. On April 1, 1972, they were ready to retire, and they put it on the market. They had a tax problem and were afraid, in case we defaulted, they would get the motel back in a dilapidated condition.

To appease the concerns, I made a daring offer. It was that we pay their asking price, but in place of a down payment, we would instead spend that $50,000 on remodeling the entire structure and we would rename it to be the Ambassador Motor Inn. From there, we would continue making payments to Edna Morris through the following year. So, in lieu of a down payment to her, we would refurbish the motel for us. Frank about fell off his chair. But the offer was approved. In the end, when we finished, we had a structure that was like a new motel. And on May 30, 1975, we hired Bill and Carole Howell to manage the Ambassador.

Herk's Motel – EconoMart – Firehole Fill up

One day in 1974, Herk Rightenour, owner of Herk's Motel and West Yellowstone Lumber, came to see me. Herk was aging and apparently was in financial trouble. He asked if I could help him out by buying his two corner lots. I told him I would check with the bank and see if I could do it.

We were able to get the money and in 1975 started to build the original EconoMart. Husky oil was our branded supplier. The gas price when we opened was thirty-seven cents per gallon. Husky eventually stopped supplying in our area, so we switched over to Phillips 66. Gas prices soared to $1.22 a gallon, and we wondered how those high prices would affect tourism.

Our daughter Stephanie and son-in-law Merrick bought the EconoMart in September of 2008 and changed the name to Firehole Fill Up.

Mountain Village Apartments – Yellowstone Arctic/Yamaha

Herk's Motel occupied the north side of the property. My first experience moving buildings occurred after buying Herk's property. We tore down some of the old cabins and relocated others to provide employee housing.

Moving buildings must have been in my blood, like it was in my dad's, because this was just the beginning. Over the years, I moved three cabins from town to the Parade Rest Guest Ranch, one cabin from the KO-Z Motel to Lapp's Cabins, and three more cabins from town to the ranch for employee housing. I also moved a four-unit motel, the house we bought from Gus Tureman, a 1903 executive rail car and the two-story cinder block Ambassador Motel, which was extremely heavy. The last moves were to make space for the new Holiday Inn, to be mentioned later.

When it came time to develop a spot for a snowmobile building, I moved more cabins off the lot. On the south half of the back lot, behind the Econo Mart, we built the Yellowstone Arctic/Yamaha, our dealership and repair shop. From here, we operated over 200 rental snowmobiles, which, to our knowledge, constituted the largest fleet of rental snowmobiles in the world.

It was obvious that we needed to provide housing for our employees. We moved the rest of the cabins off the lot south of Yellowstone Arctic/Yamaha and while the fires of Yellowstone were burning in 1988, built Mountain Village Apartments.

First Security Bank – Yellowstone Tour and Travel

West Yellowstone did not have a bank until 1966 when Mike Wilson built First Security Bank, the A-framed building next to Three Bear Lodge. I helped him finish the building the first summer Linda and I worked for him.

After the 10-year lease was up, the bank built the current public library building. We purchased the A-frame from Mike and began Yellowstone Tour and Travel. This entity became our marketing and reservation center for our operations. MarySue Costello became our first manager. It later morphed into the town's first full-fledged travel agency. It is still used for our marketing and reservation center for See Yellowstone Tours. They handle reservations and marketing for the lodge, snowmobile rentals, and snowcoach tours.

Big Western Pine – Yellowstone Country Inn

On December 11, 1975, with a new partnership formed between Bill Howell, my brother Sylvan, and myself, we bought Frank Turner out of the Big Western Pine Motel. Included in the purchase were the little Trails Inn Motel (now known as the Moose Creek Inn), the Rustler's Roost Restaurant, and the Arctic Cat snowmobile rentals.

Our purchase of the Big Western Pine eventually led the way for Bill and me to buy Frank's share of the Ambassador Motor Inn. This purchase took place on May 15, 1992. Later, we sold that property, and it became the Yellowstone Country Inn.

KO – Z Motel – The Bear's Den Activity Center – West Yellowstone Senior Center – Bear's Den Cinema – Three Bear Snowmobile Rentals

On July 15, 1991, we bought the KO-Z Motel from Art Whitmer and again moved cabins, some to another location.

In 1994, to accommodate our increasing demand, we built a new, large building and utilized this property for snowmobile storage and more employee housing. Our kids were teenagers at the time, and there was no place in town for the kids to just "hang out" for entertainment. We decided to incorporate a youth activity center into the building and called it the Bear's Den Activity Center. It was a great idea. It gave the kids a wholesome place to hang out. We had a pool table, table tennis, foosball, and arcade games. We also had a small kitchen for hamburgers, snack foods, and handmade milkshakes. We held dances for the kids, complete with a mirror ball and D. J. Jeff Carter painted comedy bears on the walls as a way to brighten the environment while the youth played pool and drank milkshakes. It was a great thing for the kids. And for the adult golfers in town, we even had Par-T-Golf.

However, after a couple of years, although our intentions were good, we found the local population was not large enough to support the activity center. It was a great thing but probably just before its time, so we closed that part of it down.

The original movie theater in town, The Chalet, burned in about 1981. I remember helping the fire department by dumping snow on part of the fire with my old loader. After the fire, the town folks had to go to Bozeman if they wanted to watch a movie. For about 15 years, a theater was really missed in town.

In fall 1996, we learned about a movie theater that was being torn down in Layton, Utah. We bought the used furnishings and equipment so we could bring a movie theater back. The most expensive piece of equipment was the popcorn popper at $5,000. The carpeting, floor lighting, sound curtains, chairs, movie projector, and screen were all hauled up from Utah on our flatbed trailer.

We incorporated the Bear's Den Cinema into the building, and it served the community well until the Imax Theater started to show regular movies, then we converted the theater space into four badly needed apartments.

See Yellowstone Tours

See Yellowstone Tours snowcoach operation was expanding, and I was going to build a facility on the property we owned next to the Rendezvous Ski Trail building. However, the town didn't want that and ended up buying the property from me for $100,000.00.

With that money, we formed the West Yellowstone Economic Development Council and eventually created the Buffalo Roam Project and Historical Walking Tour. Then we purchased, in 2011, what is now the Yellowstone Study Center Foundation building. This building provided a food preparation and eating area, classrooms and sleeping accommodations for up to fifty students. It was affordable for students from upper grade school through college. We have accommodated students from across the country with experiential learning opportunities in Yellowstone.

Since the sale of our property went for philanthropic purposes, it did not alleviate the need for a snowcoach facility. So, on May 10, 2006, we bought the old Westmart building on Yellowstone Avenue and converted it into our shop and storage facility for See Yellowstone Tours. That building, along with 5 snowcoaches, sadly, burned down November 5, 2019.

Fortunately, by that time, we had already purchased Yellowstone Alpen Guides in 2013, which became our headquarters for See Yellowstone Tours. We remodeled the building and added a badly needed tire store. Currently, we operate the facility as a joint venture, including the Point S Tire store on Yellowstone Avenue.

Lapp's Cabins

Another property purchase sort of landed in my lap, no pun intended. Alan Lapp came to see me and said he wanted to sell me his Lapp's Cabins. He could no longer operate it as a motel and was renting the cabins on a monthly basis. I had known Alan for many years, and we had a good relationship. He had worked for Mike Wilson even before I had. In his later years, he was the local sewer expert and reported the weather to the TV stations each day.

I agreed to buy his place, primarily for employee housing, which was becoming a more critical problem. We met with the local attorney to draft the papers. In front of me, the attorney told Alan that he should ask for more money. I indicated agreement, but Alan insisted on the original, lower price and said, "No, I want to sell it to Clyde for (and stated the amount again)."

We closed the deal on the terms he wanted on October 1, 1991. As usual, there was a lot of work to be done. We moved another cabin onto that property from the KO-Z Motel and built another duplex cabin, and now, we have ten more employee housing units.

TWINKLE 15

Purchase and Sale of Parade Rest Guest Ranch After 42 Years

(Includes a reprint of Pebble 17)

Linda was in awe of her dad and his love for horses. From the time she rode his horse at the rodeos until his passing, horses were an important part of their lifestyle. Consequently, when the Morris's asked us if we wanted to buy Parade Rest Guest Ranch, it took just a little nudge, and she was all for it. That nudge came when Bud Morris invited us to bring our little family out and take a ride. He had a wrangler saddle up some horses, pointed us in the right direction on the trails behind the ranch, and sent us on our way. Well, that was all it took to convince Linda and I that Parade Rest should become part of our life.

I had also grown up with horses and spent the summer with our favorite one on the sheep range. Linda had a similar upbringing with horses, and we wanted to provide our kids with that same opportunity. So, putting our kids on a horse was all Bud needed to do to seal the deal, and the Ranch became ours to love for the next 42 years.

Getting our kids comfortable on a horse, however, did not come without its perils. Stephanie was on a little horse that got spooked going through some brush and started running out of her control. Another time, Brook was with us on the way back to the barn when his horse started to run ahead of us. The saddle must not have been tight enough, and it started to slip off to the side. The horse kept running, and the saddle kept slipping further and further off to the side. It was a rather funny sight, the saddle off to the side and Brook still holding on. Luckily, the gate was closed, and the horse stopped just before he let go.

Each of our kids had their own horse that we also used for dude horses. Mike was riding his rather green broke horse, and somehow got bucked off. He was pretty banged up and Shirley, our manager, took him in on her bed and took care of some bruises and pains. Rochelle could never ride because of her asthma.

We have spent many hours enjoying riding horseback. Linda and I have marveled at spectacular views, especially when riding behind the ranch near Johnson's Lake. We also have hauled horses into Yellowstone Park and rode deep into Hayden Valley to where hundreds of buffalo roamed in the summer. We have had opportunities to let our family and grandkids go riding whenever they wanted. They also have enjoyed just being with the horses and petting them. One of my favorite photos captures a horse stretching its head out so our granddaughter London could pet it.

We have hosted family reunions at the cookout facility as well as our annual Church steak fry there. At the time of this writing, while visiting Maui, my cousin, the son of Connie (our want- to-be sister) reminded us of the time they brought their whole family to the Ranch for their family reunion. These are just a few of the memories of the Ranch.

The Ranch provided us, and our guests, a respite from the outside world. It was just an eighth of a mile off 287, ten miles north of West Yellowstone. At the far west end of the ranch property, overlooking Hebgen Lake, we built our house pictured earlier.

After 42 years of owning Parade Rest Ranch, Linda and I decided it was time to sell and move on. Among the most cherished memories are of those who managed the ranch for all those years. The first ranch managers were Walt and Shirley Butcher. They were very down to earth people with Walt, and his bib overalls, and Shirley, with her outgoing personality that contrasted with the Philadelphia lawyers that they entertained. Linda loved Walt and Shirley, and they are buried in our family plot, just a mile from the ranch.

Linda's hairdresser, Marge Wanner, and her husband, Larry, came on board as the next managers for many years. With no ranch or horse experience, Marge made up for it with a firm but loving and outgoing personality. Marge was one of a kind. She could keep many balls in the air at one time and did a great job running and yet mothering the employees. But, as is the case with all of us, age creeps up, and we decided it was finally time to sell.

Quint Whitman, who had leased many horses to us over the years and whose family owned the property abutting the ranch, expressed interest in buying the ranch. It seemed to be a natural fit. Quint was friends with Rochelle and grew up in the area. He had been running horses for many years with his fall hunting camp. When Linda heard that Quint was interested, it was all over as far as searching for a buyer was concerned.

To make a long story short, we sold the ranch to Quint, effective January 1, 2022.

The sale and our feelings were perhaps best summarized in a poem I wrote, framed, and presented to Quint, entitled "Spectacular Spring."

I was awestruck, in 2016 when I wrote "Awesome Autumn," when we purchased the ranch and it is included in Pebble 17. This poem about the Ranch, expresses the passion and feelings Linda, I, and now our family have for this beautiful place.

Like bookends, I now follow it up with "Spectacular Spring," which talks about the sale of the ranch in the spring of 2021. So, again, I wrote this poem that summarizes our feelings and hung it on the wall of the Dining Room as our last expression of the sentiment we have for this wonderful place. I hope the hearts of guests and others will be warmed as they read it, as it helps to express our feelings that have now become part of its history.

SPECTACULAR SPRING 2021

(To be read in conjunction with Awesome Autumn- 1996)

This time a camera I did have as I stood amid the
cottonwoods barren of leaves,

All alone as the memories flood one last time which
causes me to grieve.

The snow off the mountains and roofs is receding,

The leaves, flowers, and grasses soon will be increasing.

'Twas 102 years ago the Rowses built the old
Homestead Cabin,

Guests still love it for the ambiance of yesteryear that
continues to happen.

I brought my little family to the Ranch, 42 years ago
for a horseback ride.

We fell in love with it so many years ago, but age is
causing us to step aside.

We have just finished 2020, the infamous year of the
sneaky virus,

It lurked everywhere, but in the wide open spaces, it
was hard to find us.

Stop at the Office for your cabin, meal, and horseback
registration,

As you offer the hustle and bustles of life, your willing
resignation.

Cross the footbridge that spans the crystal clear waters
of Grayling Creek,

Just one of many fond memories of everyone who
comes to spend a week.

After an awesome day in the mountains, even the
horses find time to take a break,

As their riders share the photos of lakes and vistas,
'twas their privilege to take.

Cook outs with cowboy steaks cooked just right and
stories to tell,
Along with three hearty meals a day, signaled by the
ringing of the dinner bell.
Seeing Yellowstone in all its splendor is such an
unusual pleasure,
Memories of wildlife, waterfalls and geysers are such
a treasure.
Standing amid the snow banks, all alone after all of
these wonderful years;
Letters from grateful guests and many employees, it
was hard to fight back the tears.
For over two long decades, Larry's loveable Marge has
been the captain;
She wrangles the help and for the guests, they make
a memorable experience to happen.
Taking up the reins will be Quint, our like-family
neighbor and good friend,
One who loves horses and has the passion to continue
on like there is no end.
But the thing most abundantly clear is, we were so
blessed by the almighty above,
To be the caretakers for over four decades, of this
place we so dearly love.

(Clyde Seely, Spring 2021)

To the casual reader, this may be just another collection of words
mounted and hung in a frame of recycled wood. To the writer, who
has written this story over the last 42 years, it has a different meaning.
When reading it to those who know me, my voice turns funny and
the words don't come out very clear. Strange, how just trying to get
the words out is as hard as keeping the tears back. Now I think of
how the wood was carefully crafted and measured just right to fit the
poem and the accompanying photos that now hang on the Dining
Room wall for all to enjoy.

SPECTACULAR SPRING

If you wish to read more about the Ranch, I am including Pebble 17 of *Opportunity Knocked in Yellowstone* for your convenience.

Pebble 17: Parade Rest Guest Ranch

The successful person has the habit of doing the things failures don't like to do. They don't like doing them either necessarily. But their disliking is subordinated to the strength of their purpose.

—Albert E. N. Gray

In October 1979, we learned that one of the jewels in the area, Parade Rest Guest Ranch, was for sale. Retirement age was creeping up on Bud and Lucille "Lu" Morris when they invited us out to have a look around and see if we were interested in purchasing the ranch. Bud must have known what it would take for us to buy it, as he had the horses saddled up and told us to take our family for a ride on the forest trails.

Prior to that time, the property was homesteaded in 1919 by Thomas W. and Katherine "Kate" Rouse. Kate's grandmother was distantly related to Abraham Lincoln and remembered sitting on his lap. This 160-acre piece of property was rather unique in that the Gallatin National Forest surrounded it on all sides.

Original homestead cabin, modernized and still used
as a guest cabin after nearly 100 years

In 1935, retiring army Major John Rodman and his wife, Marie, bought this property. Major Rodman, a veteran of World War I, began to invite some of his friends to the ranch for some good old western hospitality and seclusion. Slowly, additional cabins were built and it became a hit with his friends, and he decided to change it to a guest ranch and named it after the military term "parade rest," meaning a position of relaxed attention, hence the name Parade Rest Guest Ranch. The Rodmans were of the old west mentality and lifestyle, which included a love for guns and even a little moonshine.

Parade Rest Guest Ranch was sold to Wells "Bud" and Lucille "Lu" Morris on July 10, 1957. They owned the ranch for 22 years and operated it in a very low-key way. They advertised in one magazine; had one wrangler, a couple of housekeepers, and a cook; and owned twelve cabins, some situated right on Grayling Creek and some up on a bluff overlooking the corral area. Bill and Carole Howell were part owners with us until 2011. During this time, we thought we could broaden the appeal to clients by emphasizing more family-oriented activities and horseback riding. In order to accomplish this, we expanded the ranch, its buildings, and personnel and made it a great place for families, reunions, and groups. We have now owned Parade Rest for over 36 years.

Still drinking up the beauty and peacefulness of Parade Rest after owning it for 16 years, I was all alone and meandering around the ranch in the fall. I was struck with feelings of awe at the beauties all around me, which continued to leave indelibly imprints on my mind. Upon returning home, I wrote the following poem entitled "Awesome Autumn."

It reads:

AWESOME AUTUMN

A camera, I did not have, so words will just have to do,
As I stood amid the cottonwoods with leaves of a
    brilliant golden hue.
'Twas fall at Parade Rest Guest Ranch,
The silence broken only by the rustling of the leaves
    and a broken branch.
At my left hand stood our "black as coal" mare,
And under my right hand her little paint colt was just
    a standin' there.

The Quaking Aspen had mostly lost their leaves,
With just a little yellow left shimmering in the breeze.
Up on the hillside a jackleg fence ran way up high.
The sagebrush, grasses, and scrub oak were so colorful,
    and yet so dry.
To the East the quakies gave way to the pines,
And just to the left Hebgen Lake and Lionshead were
    just in line.
I looked on around to complete the horizon,
The mountains of Yellowstone and the grazing lands
    for many a bison.
Right in front, Grayling Creek was just a gurgling.
Where earlier this spring it had been raging and
    whirling.
Across the creek stood the old Homestead Cabin,
Standing like a sentinel and a testament of things that
    used to happen.
Now I could not help but stand in the solemnity of
    awe, of the beauty all around me just before dark,
And our privilege to live next to Yellowstone National
    Park.
Even this frame made from the handiwork of God
    and shaped by an unskilled hand,
Takes on new meaning as a product of this almost
    hallowed land.
But the thing most abundantly clear, is that we are so
    blessed by the Almighty above,
To be the caretakers for a decade or so of this place
    we so dearly love.

(Clyde Seely, October 1996)

I made a frame, as spoken of in the poem and it hangs on the wall of the dining room, where guests can relate and enjoy. "Awesome Autumn" represents the passion and feelings Linda and I have for this beautiful peaceful place. In addition to this poem, those staying at Parade Rest will find a detailed history about the ranch that I wrote in 2001.

Not mentioned so far are those same feelings we have for those who have worked at the ranch that we have come to know and appreciate. We enjoy the guests. We enjoy the staff, and we have become attached to and appreciate those who we have relied on to manage the ranch.

Our first managers were Walt and Shirley Butcher, who managed the ranch for 15 years. Walt in his bib overalls and Shirley with her blonde hair and warm personality will always have a place in our hearts. Walt and Shirley are now buried next to our family plot at the Fur Ridge Cemetery one mile east of the ranch. A framed poem hangs in the dining room that expresses our love and appreciation for them.

As has been referred to before, a wise and very successful business man told me how he became so successful; he said "I just hire people that are better than I am and then get out of their way and let them do it." That is just what I did when we hired Marge Wanner. Marge was hired as our next ranch manager. She is also a good cook and often takes her turn in the kitchen. She has been president of the chamber of commerce and chairman of the World Snowmobile Expo in West Yellowstone since its inception over 25 years ago, and, like the energizer bunny, she just keeps going and going and going. Marge is like a mom to help. She can be stern to them and yet is always compassionate. She is normally the initial contact for the guests and makes sure they feel at home in this awesome place. Larry, her husband, still works for us at Yellowstone Arctic and sometimes provides support for Marge. To them we will always be grateful.

Seely Family, after owning the Ranch for 42
years; Grayling Creek is just behind.

TWINKLE 16

Making a Dream Come True–The Holiday Inn

In the early 90's I was in Florida promoting snowmobiling at Three Bear and "Winter in Yellowstone." We were becoming the "Snowsports capital of the world," but that did nothing for the rest of the year. I thought we needed to become more of a year round town.

On that trip, I remember one night, sitting in an outdoor hot tub at a tall convention center hotel, I looked up past the tall building into the moonlit sky and thought, *'Someday it would sure be nice if we had a conference hotel in West Yellowstone.'*

People were coming in the winter, which was our intent. Now, how could we get more people to come year round and make West Yellowstone a destination town? A conference hotel, like the one I was staying in, could be the answer. It was an idea that slowly grew until I couldn't get it out of my mind.

As usual, I discussed it with Linda, but it seemed pretty farfetched. Remember, she was used to helping with calving, teaching school with a fixed income and operating a small lodge. I don't think, at the time, she thought we would have the wherewithal to build a conference hotel in our little town, let alone turn it into a reality.

Later, one evening when my partner, Bill Howell, and I were standing on the porch of the Ambassador Motor Inn, I bounced the idea off him. I don't suppose Linda and Carole were very excited about it, but it began to grow within us. We knew we needed more property in order to build the hotel so slowly we began buying up the adjoining properties down Yellowstone Avenue until we owned the entire block.

I will skip a lot of the details, but will say we had a donor all lined up to finance the project. Eventually, I got my backhoe and started to tear down the old cinder block building. Then I thought I had better check with our financier one more time and let him know we would need the money soon. To my great shock and dismay, he casually said, *"Oh my buddies and I have decided we are too old to finance such a project."* That was it. The heat was off him and we were thrown into the fiery furnace, so to speak. We had already printed and distributed the artist's rendering of the completed hotel and touting that we would be able to hold the Snowmobile Expo in it next year. Now all that was for naught. We had already checked with all the banks we knew of, and none were large enough to take on such a significant undertaking.

It is times like that when we rely on our wives for encouragement and support. We don't expect them to jump up and say, "It's okay dear, I'll do it." No, we must finish the job. But without that constant support and encouragement there would be many more failures. The old saying, "Behind every great man is a great woman," could not be truer in my case or Bill's. Perhaps it should say, "behind every great man is an even greater woman."

As history will record, the hotel was completed on time.

We moved the OSL 1903 Executive railcar and incorporated it into the new hotel as the namesake for the Oregon Sportline Restaurant complete with a banquet kitchen to cater up to 500 people. We invited the Governor to attend the open house. We had a big ice carving of the railroad car, speeches were made, and a meal served to the invited guests. It was rather impressive to be able to seat over 300 people in one room.

Clyde, Linda, Carole and Bill with ice carving of railroad car

I am sorry to say that while writing this, we received word that Carole, Bill's wife of almost 60 years, had passed away. Linda and my memories of her will always be cherished, as we have known each other and shared so many things over the years. We saw Bill shortly after and couldn't help but think of all her mannerisms that were so typical of her. She was Bill's greatest supporter and a wonderful mother to Mark and Jason.

We have been closely associated with Bill and Carole for 48 years and never had even the slightest disagreement. They were a couple that Linda and I were proud to be in business with. In my book, I state that I would entrust my life in the hands of men like Bill.

The Holiday Inn was completed in 1995. The ensuing 10 years were fraught with snowmobile controversy, and we didn't know from one year to the next if the Park would allow snowmobiles to enter. Then, we had the major fire at Three Bear that caused us to tear down and rebuild. We felt we were being spread a little thin and so decided to sell the Holiday Inn. Now we could concentrate on rebuilding the lodge that we loved so much. Linda never felt much homage to the Holiday Inn. For West Yellowstone, this was a big project and huge building. She loved the people who worked there, but she was a Three Bear girl, for that was where her heart had always been.

TWINKLE 17

The Town That Became Home–Heaven or Hell?

When Linda and I first started working at Three Bear in the summer, it was to make money so I could finish two more years at Idaho State University and get my teaching degree. During those two summers, our involvement in Three Bear was increasing and our plans began to change. The Wilsons wanted us to stay, and we began to consider continuing to work at Three Bear Lodge during the summers. Then after I received my teaching degree, I would teach school in West Yellowstone in the winter.

We now had our first little daughter, Rochelle. Three Bear would be closed during the winter and Linda would be able to stay home. Then in the summer, Linda would help at the Lodge.

While we were considering becoming more heavily involved with Three Bear, Linda was not sure about making West Yellowstone our permanent home. She was hesitant about the small school here and the long deep winters but agreed to stay, at least until our kids were in the 4th grade. Prior to this time, only grades 1-8 were available in West Yellowstone. High school students had to stay with relatives or friends elsewhere so they could attend school. For us to have a normal family life, West Yellowstone did not seem like a long term home.

After graduating from ISU, I interviewed and received my first teaching position in West Yellowstone with a salary of $5,175. A new high school had been approved and the building addition was also completed in 1966. My 6th grade classroom was located just inside the front door of the new building. When the train first started coming to town,West Yellowstone was considered to have its real beginning. Now 58 years later, high school students living in West Yellowstone could stay at home and go to school.

With a high school now in place, and me becoming familiar with the faculty and school programs, Linda's concerns began to wane. Mrs. Dunbar was an excellent librarian and English teacher, along with other great elementary and secondary level teachers. Well, time passed and before our daughter, Rochelle, was in the 4th grade, we had leased, then purchased Three Bear and there was no thought of leaving West Yellowstone. We decided that instead of just dipping our toes in the water, we needed to dive in all the way and become part of the community or it would never work.

We found there are some real advantages to attending a small school.

When our last three boys were going to grade school, Mr. Baier, their 6th grade teacher, organized an unbelievable program that taught life skills to our kids. One of the programs he organized was a school ski program with Big Sky ski hill, while it was still in its infancy . For $50.00 a winter, Big Sky would provide ski passes, complete with lessons, for a student. Our school district provided a bus every Saturday, hauling a load of school kids to and from the ski hill. I suppose there was an ulterior motive for them; if they could hook our kids on skiing, they would continue to come. Well, it worked.

Linda and I would take our kids skiing when I could. Lois Klatt, a good friend, would take her three boys with Linda and our three boys. The mothers thought they would have to go slow so their boys could keep up. Well, that was not how it worked. Lois and Linda would make it part way down the hill and all of a sudden, they would hear a loud, "Hi—Bye, Mom," as the boys swished past them, laughing. This was the beginning of a life skill that still remains. Most of our boys eventually traded skis for snowboards but still love it. In fact, Doug just returned from Japan snowboarding, where he had a super time. It all started because of Mr. Baier's program in our little grade school. Also, release time from school for cross country ski classes was granted. The Rendezvous Ski Trail, where they skied, has become an icon for cross country skiing today.

Our graduating classes of 12 to 20, I dare say, have a higher ratio of scholarship dollars per capita than any other school I know. Scholarships are available to anyone who has the desire and commitment to furthering their education in tech or college training and it is commonplace for students to be awarded upwards of $20,000. Our little school has produced doctors, lawyers, professionals in high places, and capable individuals with strong work ethics and character. All five of our kids went on to college and have made us proud. We are surely glad we did not leave West Yellowstone before they got to the 4th grade.

There is something about a small-town environment that levels the playing field. A little fish swimming in a little pond seems to gain the confidence to become a bigger fish swimming in a bigger pond. In this, who can outdo who competitive world in which we live, as Linda often says, "It's not what's on the outside, but what's on the inside that really counts."

Linda reminds me that there is a saying that has gone around town for years, "West Yellowstone is a man's heaven and a woman's hell." That was the impression many had.

Men, for the most part, love it here. Besides great employment opportunities, activities abound in and around West Yellowstone. Hunting, fishing, hiking, boating and cool summers are here for the sportsman. Winter is a bit more challenging, but the deep snow provides great snowmobiling and cross country skiing on the Rendezvous Ski trails and into Yellowstone. These are just some of the reasons why West Yellowstone is considered a "man's heaven" and men want to live here.

Women moving in from the outside, leaving the *everything at your fingertips* world, are not always so enamored. The cold, deep winters, the lack of big box stores, and the long distances to almost anywhere can be some legitimate concerns. Initially, Linda was not willing to commit to a long-term relationship with this little town of about 600 residents. For some, isolation took its toll, and many did not stay long. On the other hand, many people also loved it here. Some of the reasons that some men love it are also the same reasons why some women love it. But regardless of gender, it seems the most important reason people live here is because *of* the people that live here.

There is something about this place that grows on you. Soon the town, the people, and the church affiliations start to connect residents to a feeling of *home*. For Linda, in just a few short years, she became part of this little town, and this little town became a part of her. Sixty years later, when we now have the means to move to warmer and larger communities, we have no desire to do so. West Yellowstone is embedded in us, and we are embedded in the town. It turns out that we are not alone in our love for West Yellowstone. Many friends and acquaintances, both men and women, agree this is home. After all, "home is where the heart is," and consequently, our heart is here.

Now we have friends who moved here to retire so they can enjoy the very things that some run away from, which shows it all depends on what drives a person from the inside.

TWINKLE 18

The Reciprocating Benefits of Church Affiliation

Since the outset, the church has been a mainstay for us and certainly added to the "this is home" feeling. We have always been active in the Church of Jesus Christ of Latter-day Saints. The feelings of camaraderie among those we have known for so many years is cherished by us.

Linda and I would bring all five of our little kids to church. Keeping them quiet, so as not to disturb others, was a real problem. Since I was in a leadership position in the church for almost 14 years I would have to sit on the stand and conduct the meetings while Linda was in the audience keeping all under control. Stephanie was born when I was first put in as Branch President. The three boys were yet to be born. As they came along, Rochelle and eventually Stephanie would help keep them entertained. I was released as Branch President when Stephanie was almost 14 years old. And that is not all.

In addition to the time spent wrangling five little children in church, Linda basically took care of them by herself all day on Sunday. At that time, we had meetings in the morning, and then I would go to stake meetings in St. Anthony every Sunday, a 150-mile round trip. While I was driving 600 miles per month to St. Anthony, or 7200 miles per year, Linda was taking care of our two girls and three boys at home. How many hours does it take to drive 7200 miles? Add to that, the time spent in the West Yellowstone meetings and the St. Anthony meetings, and the time spent on other ecclesiastical responsibilities in West Yellowstone, and she spent a lot of time alone with the kids, without a complaint. Basically, I was almost an absentee dad on Sundays for 14 years.

In 1982, after I was released and put on the Ashton High Council, Linda was called to be the Ashton Idaho Stake Relief Society President. I told the kids that with her new calling in the Stake, she would be gone quite a lot and that she needed our support. Little Brook asked, "Does that mean we have to cry a lot?" In our monthly testimony meeting, whenever Linda spoke from the pulpit, she would often cry when she was expressing her deep convictions about church teachings and her love toward family and friends. I suppose he thought that we all had to do the same to support her.

With our new callings, both Linda and I had to travel to Ashton regularly. Sometimes we could correlate our meetings but often we had to go at different times.

The Relief Society is the women's organization in the church. Among other things, it deals with helping those in need and providing leadership and spiritual development. The Relief Society has always been near and dear to Linda's heart. Perhaps this love is a carryover from her grandmother, both she and my own grandmother worked together for 19 years preparing bodies for burial.

Like most organizations there is a presidency. Linda has been a counselor to several presidents and was now called to be the president of the Ashton Idaho Stake Relief Society. She received a letter from the General Presidency (Barbara Smith, President) in Salt Lake, February 4, 1982. She was congratulated for being called and was given instructions and responsibilities.

This required her driving to Ashton often, where she would preside and conduct the affairs. I was told by one of her counselors, she oversaw the largest Stake Relief Society dinner ever held. Another counselor shared that Linda was truly Christ-like, always putting others first. I believe that Linda was an embodiment of Matt 23-11, "But he that is greatest among you shall be your servant."

In connection with her callings in the church, she frequently was asked to teach and speak. She spoke to the stake youth group about marriage. She also shared tributes about three aunts and an uncle at their funerals. Her role as President of the Stake Relief Society involved multiple teaching, speaking, and presiding assignments, requiring her to travel to meetings from Chester to West Yellowstone.

After being released from her stake position, she was called to be the West Yellowstone Relief Society President. She loved that calling and the women she served. Stephanie has said, "Mom was an example to me of how to fulfill church callings and to be an active member of the ward." Stephanie has followed in her mother's footsteps and is serving, as her mother did, with the same service-minded love.

I mention this because many of those who are from around town and in our businesses would not know about this side of Linda. She has the ability to communicate from the heart. She really does care about others. She does not push herself to be in front of others, however, when asked to perform a leadership or teaching role, she does it very well.

When it was time to build the new church, we had to figure out a way to raise enough money to pay for our local share. We would have dinners every month where the women would bring the food and then we would turn around and pay to eat it. We have often said, "We almost ate our way into the new church."

Another way of raising money was for the Relief Society to quilt beautiful hand-stitched quilts all year long and then in the spring have a quilt sale. Not only did this raise money for the church, it developed strong friendship ties between the women. I referred to them as the Quilting Queens. They made everything from baby quilts to fancy prize-winning quilts. Quilting groups served a twofold purpose: producing a useful item and socializing with the latest news, such as "Have you heard . . .?"

The Quilting Queens
From left to right:Alice Waldron, Linda Seely, Lois McCray, Donna Schaap,
Helene Rightenour, Norman Martin and Linda Burke

Lois was the most prolific quilter and won prizes at the Blackfoot, Idaho State Fair. Donna Schaap took up the reins as leader of the group when Lois left. Since Bill passed away, she is continuing at her home, making grandbaby quilts to help occupy her time.

As the years continue to pass, some of the old stalwarts have moved on to new addresses or on to the other side. One by one, they are leaving until now the group may no longer be quilting in the church. They are ending a legacy for so many, the joy of having "a quilt that Grandma gave me."

Quilting is the term given to the process of joining a minimum of three layers of fabric together by stitching manually using a needle and thread. I suppose many quilts were brought across the plains. Seldom was a piece of used fabric ever thrown away. It could be reused to cut squares or many other shapes and stitched together to make not only very warm and functional but some elegant-looking quilts.

One of the gifts that Mike and Frances Wilson gave us was an Alaskan Chilkat Indian blanket that still hangs in Three Bear Lodge. It is 80+ years old. These have been made for hundreds of years. The craft of making these beautiful ceremonial blankets is now a lost art because it was not passed on to or future generations weren't interested in learning such things.

Someday, our little quilting group may dwindle, and the art of quilting may be lost. However, we still use a quilt given to us before we were married by Linda's dear Aunt Blanche. It is still on our bed after 60+ years. One of the reasons it is still being used is because of its sentimental value. There are many cherished quilts out there that will also be in existence for decades to come.

TWINKLE 19

Putting Others First

"*Well, that is just the way I have always been.*"

—Linda

*Teddy Roosevelt once said, "Nobody cares how much
you know until they know how much you care."*

Linda seems to have a driving force from within to make others feel good by building them up. At church, with a twinkle in her eye, she will bend over to talk to the little kids. She compliments mothers on how cute their kids are. She looks up to the basketball-aged kids and talks to them and lets them know she is watching and rooting for them. Now, after church, I see one of those boys make a bee line over to Linda to give her a big hug.

Recently, on our way to Maui for our annual retreat, two little boys were deplaning with their parents. Linda bent over and looked them in the eye and said she had noticed that they were such well-behaved boys. They and their mother beamed and a conversation ensued. The mother had homeschooled her boys and was pleased with the compliment.

I remembered back 40+ years ago when we first took our little family of five to Maui for the first time. The three little boys had shirts alike along with Stephanie and Rochelle. More than once, someone commented, both in the terminal and airplanes, what a nice little family we had. It was sort of unusual to see five little kids all together on an airplane. I know it pleased us and made us feel rather proud of them.

Rochelle, Mike, Brook, Doug, Stephanie
One of our first trips to Hawaii about 42 years ago

Linda has always made our kids' friends feel welcome in our home. We lived on, literally, the other side of the tracks, so to speak, that was until the train tracks were removed between our house and the rest of the town. Our kids had the forest in the back and train tracks in the front of the house on which to play. The boys and friends found round pieces of metal left from the trains that they called train money. They would also build forts in the forest behind our backyard.

The girls, Rochelle and Stephanie had their friends, Anita and Heidi, respectively, over to build a greenhouse in the back yard or just spend a lot of time in the house. Little friends seemed to gravitate to our house and Linda was always one to make them feel at home. They knew they were welcome to get in the fridge whenever they wanted. Brook said he used her as an example when he was raising London. He said, "I wanted her friends to feel that way when they came to our house to see London."

A close friend of Linda's was her hairdresser, Dianne Job. She became very ill with cancer and before she died, asked Linda if she would take care of her son, Ryan (Bezzer to us). After her passing, Bezzer, who was already a friend with our boys, moved in with us. He finished school, went on a mission, and has also become as though he were part of the family. Some of Stephanie's and the boy's friends refer to Linda as their second Mom. Currently a youth has referred to Linda as his third grandma.

She has had a profound impact on not only her kids but so many others. As mentioned elsewhere, after a friend passed away, a post was found in which he mentioned the most inspirational people in his life. Only five were listed: his parents, his grandparents on his mother's side, and Linda Seely.

Linda has influenced people in many ways that she will never know. But recently, we had one special reminder about her influence on students when she taught school in St. Anthony and we were preparing to be married.

My niece Lynne, daughter to my sister Norma, was at the Parker, Idaho Cemetery paying respects to her mother when a woman standing at a nearby grave introduced herself as Linda Miller. She had seen Lynne next to Seely's headstones so she asked if Lynne knew a Linda Seely. Turns out her father was taught by Linda in the eighth grade in St. Anthony. He liked Linda as a teacher—and he liked her name which is how his daughter was named Linda. It was uncanny his daughter Linda (Miller) was talking to Lynne, who is Linda's (Seely) niece. What a coincidence that day.

She is always concerned about others and doesn't want to put anyone out. This morning, for example, she was worrying about asking someone to do something for her. I was sure they would be glad to do it and not think it was an imposition. I said, "Well, perhaps you shouldn't try to pre-guess what someone else is thinking, I'm sure they would be glad to help."

She said, **"Well, that is just the way I have always been. I don't want to put other people out."**

This has always been the case. Even now in our older years, when it is perfectly permissible for others to wait for us to go first, there is always a "you go first" competition. Throughout our 60 years of marriage, whether it's driving or sharing snacks at home, Linda has always offered me the first bite and insisted that I have the last one.

As time passed, so did the ages of our kid's friends but Linda's acceptance of them never changed. Here are a few examples:

When Brook told us about a friend in West Yellowstone with vision problems, Linda didn't hesitate. She scheduled an eye doctor appointment in Bozeman, accompanied this friend, and ensured he got fitted with contact lenses.

Oceas needed some money desperately and reached out to Brook, wondering if we would lend him some money. He asked, and Linda provided the help he needed. Oceas has gone through some tough times but made it, and now he has a family of his own. He still thinks Linda is the coolest mom ever.

The age of the friends didn't make any difference. During his early twenties, Brook sometimes brought some rather sketchy, friends to stay overnight. Later these friends commented, and still do, how welcome Linda made them feel.

Steven Redwine, one of Brook's friends, was a teenage boy who spent the winter nearly alone in West Yellowstone. One evening, at about zero degrees, he knocked at the door. There he stood with a pretty poinsettia he had carried across town for Linda for Christmas.

Linda and all of us thanked him for it. Then Linda hurriedly took it into the other room for it was frozen stiff. Soon it thawed and wilted, although Steven never knew. Linda must have been a special person for a teenage boy, from a troubled background to spend his money, scarce as it was, to make such an effort to give thanks to a woman he undoubtedly cared for greatly.

It was several years later when Brook, Linda and I stopped at the Soledad State Prison in California to see Steven. Apparently, things had gotten worse.

Linda possesses an innate gift of being able to strike up conversation with anyone. Whether it is little kids in church or parents of a little family, she has something nice to say to them. She likes everyone and in return they like her. She has never spoken bad about any of the kids' friends. She really tries to encourage and lift them to new heights. When she does, they reciprocate with increased affection and respect. Many have shared how she has been a shining example to them of what a mom and parent should be.

Remembering causes us to preserve the memory

To remember our loved ones reinforces our love for them. To be remembered by those we love, in a way, expresses their love by recalling memories of us. It is an unexpected paycheck to be remembered for being kind, considerate, helpful, caring, and for giving of love to them in the first place.

This is especially true with our kids and grandkids. They remember the little incidental things from a different perspective than non-family members. I will relay a few little memory snippets that have endeared Linda to them.

Mike and Michelle's family (Eric, Nate and Lena), said they want Grammy to know how much they love her. She carries a loving light with her wherever she goes. They love her hugs, and she always makes them feel better when they are around her. They just wish they could spend more time with her, even if she continues to ask them to put their phone away so they would just talk to her. Grammy is always comforting and fun to be around. They love her joking around with them when they are just hanging out together.

They shared, *"Grammy is a caring, patient, and loving person who always makes us feel part of the family. She is one of their favorite people to be around. She's our cool grandma who's always got cookies or snacks for us."*

We recently returned from Maui with Doug's family. Ben said he loves it when Grammy tells him that he should pursue something that he likes to do. He loves it when she pulls him up close and shakes her finger at him and tells him he has a lot of ability and that he can go far, if he will make up his mind to do it. I witnessed this very thing as we were saying goodbye before departing from Maui, she took him by the arm and said that whatever he decided to do, he could do it. Then she shared that she had faith in him and that she would pray for him. All of this she said with a determined look, but also with a twinkle in her eye.

Kate loves it when she sees her, pulls her up close, looks her in the eye, and with a kiss on the cheek, tells Kate how proud she is of her.

Ila said, *"Grammy pampers me by saying, 'Oh, let me do that for you.'"And she does."*

Stephanie and her family, Shelby, Kelsey, Drake and Parker recalled memories of their Mom and Grammy, special things she may have done unintentionally or just because she loves them.

Linda has never bragged about her cooking; in fact, she would have most believe that she was not good at it. But our family says it differently. Stephanie and our grandkids reminded us of her famous German raisin cookies, her chocolate fluff dessert, and three ingredient fudge. They loved coming to our house for Sunday dinner.

They also mentioned our Thanksgiving dinners during their growing up years in which Linda cooked for upwards of fifty people.

Everyone loves her chicken and noodles on mashed potatoes, and hotcakes with homemade syrup made from the chokecherries picked straight from our front porch.

They remember our Mother's Day picnics at the 7-mile bridge and at Denny Creek.

Stephanie looked forward to the school shopping trips with Mom and Rochelleand sometimes Heidi. These were normally to Salt Lake. Later, Shelby and Kelsey also remember those shopping trips. The thing that has always amazed me is after all her enjoyable time on those shopping trips, how few things she actually bought for herself. She was a shopping queen that sometimes came home without anything.

Linda got hooked on Tab and later Diet Coke. It had to have ice! Then she would sit and watch TV with a magazine in her lap. The doctor suggested that she stop drinking soda, and I still cannot see how she can read a magazine and watch TV at the same time. Although one of the few shows she does not read during is "Blue Bloods."

Riding bikes in the summer has already been mentioned by all, which often ended up at Eagles with a chocolate soda.

She was their biggest cheerleader at our grandkid's games, and they could pick out her voice, even in a crowd.

Of her, they said, "Grammy is loving, kind, caring, compassionate, funny, and tells you *how it is* and is not afraid to be honest. She is a true blooded Aggie and helped all four of us become one too! She has been such a big part of our lives and has been there for so many of the daily things throughout our growing up years. Our everyday memories include our Grammy in the little things of life and we wouldn't want it any other way."

Thanksgiving–A Family Tradition

Some of the most cherished memories made were around the special Thanksgiving traditions that filled our home.

The first winter we lived in West Yellowstone, the family decided it would be fun to spend Thanksgiving in West Yellowstone with us. Linda was rather intimidated to cook dinner for all the Seely family. We bought a large turkey and Mother brought along her steamer to make her special dry dressing. The rest of the family brought side dishes and desserts and dinner turned out really perfect. Linda was really quite relieved.

I decided to rent two double track Ski Doo snowmobiles that we could take the little kids for a ride after dinner. All of this was just the start of a family tradition that carried on for 37 years and grew from about 20 to 54 people.

First we hosted the family in our apartment, then our house on Obsidian Avenue, and finally in our new log home at the Ranch.

Snowmobiles were waiting to be ridden after dinner. We always said it took hours to prepare dinner and only minutes to eat it because everyone was anxious to go on the annual snowmobile ride.

Since we went into the snowmobile rental business, we could provide snowmobiles and clothing for all. It was quite an undertaking to get all the little kids and adults outfitted in the right-sized clothing and assigned to snowmobiles. On that ride, I felt like a mother hen as I guided about thirty snowmobiles with drivers of all ages.

Through the years that followed, we always started out for Two Top Mountain but seldom made it, as there were always a few mishaps with the teenagers and my two older slowpoke sisters. We also let the sun determine how far we went, since it got cold quickly after that. Plus once the call of turkey leftovers and homemade pies began to beckon that Linda had waiting for us, we heeded the call and turned back for home. Each year, all the relatives looked forward to coming. And upon returning home, none of their friends could top the stories shared about our Seely family thanksgivings in Yellowstone.

We started out with our young, small immediate family but the invitation grew to include a large, extended family. By now, the little families have grown in numbers, and after 37 years, it became time for them to share their families with their in-laws and start their own Thanksgiving traditions and. Still today, they comment on how

Linda put it all together and how much they enjoyed "Thanksgiving in Yellowstone" for all those years.

Key Chains: A Traveling Memory Tradition

When visitors come to the house, there is a certain place they always pause to look at a wall of bright, glistening key chains. Let me explain. Years ago, while on various trips together, we always wanted to bring home a memento. One of the most common identifiable items, with mention of the name and fame of a certain place, was a key chain.

We began collecting keychains from our travels in foreign lands, placing them in a small bucket. Eventually the "cup runneth over," so to speak. To address this, I took reclaimed darkened wood, measuring 4 feet by 5 inches and hammered in two rows of little inconspicuous nails every two inches. We hung a souvenir keychain on each nail and created a pretty display that we attached to our log wall. As we traveled more, we continued to collect more keychains. Then our kids and grandkids picked up on the idea as an easy memento from their travels.

As everyone continued to travel, I increased the number of boards on the wall. Now there are five boards with 335 keychains, from all over the world. With the ceiling light shining down on these colorful keychain mementos, it is rather striking and causes one to remember where they bought that one, for Grammy. It has been a wonderful thing to have it visually, in front of us, as we remember the places we have been and the places our family have thought of us while they were traveling. And, once again, it is time to add another board.

Linda's keychain collection

TWINKLE 20

The Loss of Our Granddaughter, London

(Includes a reprint of Pebble 33)

Linda lost her father when he was only forty-six-, daughter Rochelle when she was twenty-nine, her brother, Norman and her granddaughter London when she was just thirteen. In 1 Corinthians 15:55, it asks, *"O death, where is thy sting?"*

Linda grieved over the loss of her dad, in those early years, with only a limited understanding of what death brings. In our church, the first Sunday of the month, a testimony meeting is held in which anyone can go to the pulpit and bear their testimony of the Savior and how he has affected their life. Two weeks after Rochelle died, I remember standing and saying that I knew more surely now than before her death that God lives and that because of Christ, we would see her again. We also had our children and family members from which to gain strength and encouragement.

When London, Brook's daughter died, she was an only child and he a single parent. You will read more about her, both in her life sketch, in this Twinkle and again in Pebble 33. Brook has since immersed himself in the scriptures and other writings. He is totally at peace with her loss. Around every corner are vivid memories of her, happy memories. But he knows her loss is only temporary. Like Linda, who still feels her own mother's presence, Brook believes that the veil is thin and that London is near. God had a reason for calling her home.

"O, death, where is thy sting?" Though we all miss her, the sting is replaced by sweet memories, and knowing that the Savior died that we might all live again and will see her in just *'the twinkling of an eye.'*

Linda said that London was cute from the day she was born. She had a cute smile and a captivating personality. She had an infectious giggle, enhanced whenever she was with her friends. London stole our hearts with her cheerful and happy voice. Whenever she was around her friends, she seemed to be the catalyst for getting everybody involved.

She loved to cook, and sometimes she would let us know that she was cooking dinner for us. She timed everything so it would be finished at the same time.

London's bed in Salt Lake was just against a sheetrock wall. Surely, she would like a headboard. So, Grandpa started to build her one out of reclaimed wood. When she came to visit us, she was able to assist in making it. She was happy with it and proud she had been able to help.

London helping make her own headboard

While she was there, Grandpa inscribed on the back, the photo shown here. Little did we know that this expression of love would turn into a memorial within just 3 months.

Back of headboard,
Engraved expression of love

Too often when loved ones pass away, we regret that more endearment had not been expressed. That was not the case with London. Instead, she stated that love to her dad in this note, given exactly two years to the day before she passed away.

Dear Dad   *Nov. 19, 2019*

Have I ever told you how grateful I am for everything you do for me? Thank you for all the memories we have. Thank you for taking me on trips like Yellowstone and Hawaii. Thank you for teaching me how to write my name. Thank you for our house and for my own room. And finally for taking my friends to wherever we want.

Thank you for being the best dad ever. Thanks for being fun to talk to. This is why we have so many memories, it's because we actually talk.

Thanks for teaching me how to write my name. I love the first time I wrote my name on a paper. It is so cute.

Thank you for a house, and my room with everything I have ever wanted.

Thank you for taking me to all kinds of places like Canada, California, Yellowstone and Hawaii . . .

I love you so much and I've also said thanks so many times, but THANKS.

Love, London

Then came that unforeseen night that changed the lives of so many. At 11:00 PM, because London had a pain in her neck, Brook took her to the LDS hospital. By 2:00 AM, they transferred her to the Primary Children's Hospital. Surely, this was just a temporary scare and they would find the problem. However, each day went by slowly as the doctors were chasing one symptom after another. Whatever was wrong seemed to be playing hide and seek with the doctors, and in just 5 days, as healthy as she was, she was gone.

Fox 13 News, in Salt Lake, did a special on London in which her friends at Clayton School and her dad were interviewed. It was very touching.

The funeral was huge. They had to set up chairs all the way to the very back of the cultural hall. At the funeral, London's aunts Shelby and Kelsey read the following life sketch:

London Eliza Seely was born at St. Mark's Hospital in Salt Lake City on a day we will never forget! August 8th, 2008, to Brook and Erin. It was that day 8-8-08, that all of our lives were changed for the better. London not only stole the hearts of her parents but everyone she met with her big brown eyes, amazingly curly hair, the cutest grin, accompanied by the world's best giggle.

She graduated from the Little Leopard's Preschool at East High School in 2011 and Ensign Elementary in the spring of 2020. London attended Clayton Middle School through 7th Grade and was currently enrolled in 8th grade.

London loved going to school and being with her friends. She volunteered at her elementary school and always loved helping other children feel welcome. If someone didn't have a friend to sit with at lunch, she was the first to invite them to sit with her and her friends. When London got into Clayton Junior High she bloomed. She was outgoing and charismatic and made friends with so many. She was a giver—she was always known to have a piece of gum on hand to give to classmates. She would freely offer to purchase treats at Harmon's after school for friends who didn't bring their wallet. Her dad specifically remembers times when she had been given a gift, and within a week, she had given it to someone else. London was always very caring and would be the first to help if anyone she cared for was physically or emotionally hurt. She has always been very in-tune with understanding emotions and listening. These qualities made her a loving and compassionate friend.

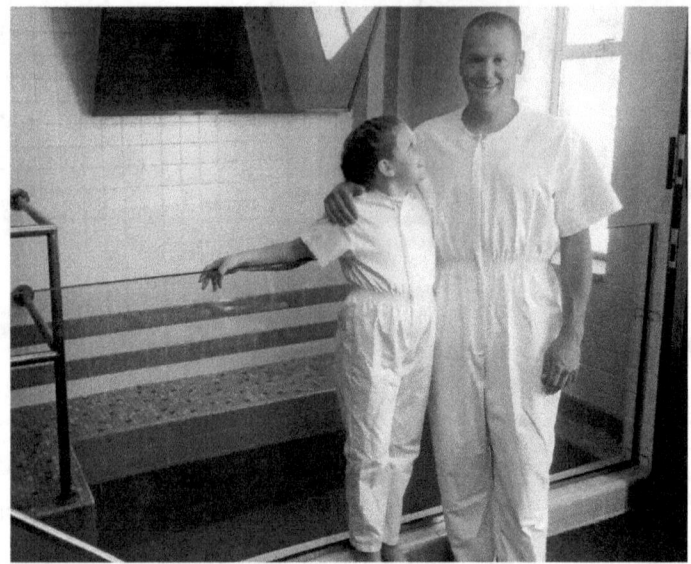

London's baptism.
Happy day for father and daughter

London was a member of the Church of Jesus Christ of Latter-day Saints and was baptized by her dad on September 10, 2016. She enjoyed attending her youth group activities. She had recently gained an interest in family history and genealogy work. She loved the gospel and was a great example of Christlike service and love to all of her member and non-member friends. Many people were drawn to London due to her spirit and the light of Christ that she always carried with her!

London loved to cook and bake. She would try new recipes and practice making them with her own spin and flavors, she could make a mean salad that would satisfy any vegetarians needs. She loved to make cakes and cookies and give them to friends and neighbors. She was able to make many friends through this act of service.

London in London

When she was 9 years old, she spent part of her summer in London, England. It was there that she was able to create numerous memories in the city that was named after her. Her and Brook got to explore the city to its fullest and she even got to visit the mission home where Brook had spent so much time when he was in the mission field.

London loved to go camping and adventuring with family and friends. London is very well traveled and has been to more places in her 13 years than most travel in a lifetime. Some of London's favorite places to visit were Maui, London, California, and visiting her grandparents in Yellowstone. In fact, her friends and cousins remember spending time with London on many fun-filled trips to Yellowstone. Brook would graciously pack up his car along with 3 to 5 kids to drive the 5 hours to Yellowstone. These car rides were full of singing. Assuming Brook is a NSYNC fan, I am sure he loved listening to them sing "I want it that way" at the top of their lungs on repeat.

Much to her father's dismay, London was an animal lover, especially when it came to dogs! Whether it was her pet fish calendar, whose life was dramatically taken by the kitchen garbage disposal; her dog, Lambbear, who was her snuggle buddy; or her grandparents dog, Camo, who was the best sledding partner, she had a big soft spot in her heart for all things that were furry, fuzzy, and four-legged.

She was very creative and loved making things with her hands. When she was little, she would spend hours and hours painting, drawing, or doing any arts and crafts. London would always try and convince her dad to take her and her friends to paint pottery and make slime, as no other parent wanted to deal with that mess. She also was known for the best tie-dye shirts in town. In fact, this past summer London custom made over 300 tie-dye shirts for a nonprofit. She also had made plans to work at the Yellowstone T-Shirt Shop this coming summer to further express her creativity and expand her Yellowstone t-shirt collection.

She loved to garden with her great grandma in Logan. She would grow her own veggies at home and became very good at growing her own succulents in her kitchen window.

Every year, she and her dad had a Lagoon pass and would often just go for a few rides before bed! She also loved to go with friends and cousins. Her and her friends would sometimes have contests of how many times they could go on cannibal in a row without getting sick. I think the running number was 12, clearly, she didn't suffer from motion sickness.

London loved tradition. One of her favorite holidays was 4th of July. Every year she could not wait to celebrate with her Seely family in Yellowstone. Whether it was the fireworks, riding in the parade on floats made by Grandpa, the veggie burgers cooked by Steve Garner or her uncle Merrick, or just hanging out with her cousins, London made sure, even if it meant convincing her mom, that she got to celebrate the 4th in West Yellowstone. London also had a tradition of picking out a Christmas tree with her dad during the holiday season in Yellowstone! She enjoyed winter sports which included snowboarding, snowmobiling, skiing, and ice skating.

In the summer she enjoyed skateboarding. She had a skateboard basically from the time she could stand on her own two feet. Whether she was riding it barefoot, in a tutu and butterfly wings, or down the streets of the avenues, it was something that bonded her and her dad from the very beginning, and I think it's safe to say that it is probably one of Brook's proudest dad moments.

A few more summer activities she enjoyed were swimming, fishing at Hebgen Lake, riding horses, and picking/growing flowers. These are just a few of London's favorite hobbies and traditions. She was adventurous, easy going, free-spirited, and always lived life to the fullest. London was loved by everyone!

London's reach was beyond what we could ever fathom. She touched the lives of so many she met. London taught us valuable lessons on how to love and live carefree and happy. She will always be remembered by her fun-loving bouncy personality and her distinct giggle that could light up ANY room. London Eliza, you will be dearly missed.

Pebble 33: Loss of Our Granddaughter

"I miss your dear kind face and loving way . . . And yet dear heart, I know that God is just. I know he called you home because he must and I can only wait and pray and trust."

—The above was taken from her Greatgrandmother Seely's Book of Remembrance and read at London's funeral.

Death is no stranger to any of us. I tell the following, so many can relate to such sorrowful times and may find some comfort. It has now been twenty-nine years since we lost our 29-year old daughter, Rochelle. (See Pebble 11.) We hoped we would never have to experience such a loss again. However, this year she was followed by our 13-year-old granddaughter, London Seely. London's father, our son Brook, lives in Salt Lake City. He was a single father and had shared 50/50 custody of his only daughter, London, for about 11 of those years.

In speaking at her funeral, I referred back to my experience as a boy with the pebbles I would throw in the pond and how I would watch the ripples spread out across the water. That memory became a metaphor for my life which followed. The ripples caused by the pebbles were the influences others had on me and I had on others.

London, on the other hand, had two pebbles and two worlds. In one end of the pool her pebble influenced her mother and the world around her. In the other end of the pool her pebble influenced her father, Brook, and the world around him. Skillfully, she navigated between each of those two worlds.

I would like to talk about London's ripples in the pool in which I knew her.

She loved to laugh and giggle. I can envision her learning how to ride her first bike without training wheels, skateboarding, swimming, trips to Maui, and to the city that could well be named after her, LONDON.

London and Brook visited us often, where she progressed from corral rides to riding her own horse at Parade Rest, from riding behind her wild and crazy dad on a snowmobile to driving her own to Two Top Mountain at Yellowstone, and sharing all of this world with her friends, all with her dad.

He has immortalized her at their home at 173 J St. with things she had drawn or made. It is almost like a shrine of London by a dad whose world revolved around no other.

Brook was a father whose main purpose in life was that of being a good Dad. He traded his work shifts with others so he could always be with her on his week.

London was a healthy, happy girl, then one night she complained of a pain in her neck and Brook took her to the hospital. Five surreal days later, on November 19, 2021, she was gone.

Brook was not one to cry. In fact, I have never seen him cry with broken bones or individual sorrows. At his Sister Rochelle's death, even though he tried and tried, he just couldn't get the tears to flow that came so naturally to others. London grew up knowing that about her father. Then one night, as he was alone with London, amid the tangle of life support equipment hooked up to her, he leaned over her and with new and unfamiliar tears running down his cheeks, he choked out the words, "London, you have taught me how to cry."

Within hours she was gone. Tears were shed and words too tender and emotional to share here were uttered as he shared his innermost thoughts with us.

Now we come to the nagging question—**Why**, after only 13 years was she taken? What sense can be made of that? I guess it is easy to feel that we are denied and maybe even cheated, for not being given the right to see London grow into adulthood. But our vision is blurred—in fact, partially limited during our mortal existence and we must put our faith in God, Our Father in Heaven, and His plan. It would be easy to become bitter to blame someone, or to think we are being punished for something we had done.

But we should not, cannot do that. All mortals are subject to premature death, or suffering, or disease, or accidents.

Death is an inescapable happening for each of us. It cannot always be in a timely fashion or when we would choose it to happen. If that were so (with our limited knowledge), we would choose never to have loved ones die, and thus thwart the plan of God. That plan places death as one of the blessed conditions that is a necessary happening prior to eternal life. So, although we mourn for a time, the passing of our sweet London will only be a temporary parting.

In Ecclesiastes 3 it tells us, "To everything there is a season, and a time to every purpose under the heaven: 2. **A time to be born, and a time to die,** etc."

London's passing is a personal confirmation to that. London was a healthy, happy girl and one week later, she was gone. Brook kept us informed as he took her to the LDS Hospital and then transferred her by ambulance to the renowned Primary Children's Hospital. Each day she declined one step at a time. The team of doctors would think it was one thing and then something else. It was almost like it, whatever it was, was playing hide and seek with the doctors. And each time, a downward step was taken. Test after test was given until, after only 5 days, she passed away with them not knowing the cause.

I believe that was a confirmation of Spencer W. Kimball's statement that "we may bring on death prematurely, but that we seldom can exceed our time to be called back home by very much." Surely, it was London's time. There is no doubt in my mind that her work was finished here and that God needed her there more than we do here.

The death of our daughter Rochelle was also way too early. (I hoped that I would never have to go through something like this again.) We also wondered, **why?**

At that time, someone sent us a card with a statement that still hangs on our refrigerator. It says (refer to page 99): "Never put a question mark where the Lord puts a period."

We went through a similar time of mourning and questioning. Later, when I was preparing a talk, Psalms 46:10 stood out, which said, **"Be still,** and know that I am God." That seemed a little harsh. But I have grown to love that verse. In our limited understanding of the eternal scheme of things, it is easy to question, to criticize, to worry, to be impatient. "Be still, **and know that I am God,"** is comforting to me and means, no need to worry and question, it's going to be alright. I've got your back, so to speak, It will all work out.

Today we mourn the loss of London and we will miss her. There will always be a hole in our hearts. We have been heartbroken with the loss of our granddaughter. Why did this happen and how can we reconcile our grief with peace, hope, and the courage to go on?

Well, since death is as universal and as certain as birth, it is inevitable that we will all, at some time, suffer from the sorrow of parting and being left behind. Perhaps we would postpone death if we could, but no matter how long we live, sooner or later, either we leave those we love or they leave us. This, we all accept as an inescapable condition of this life.

But in accepting it, we need not accept it as final, as the ultimate end of our existence. For this, we are grateful for that first Easter when Christ, after having been born and lived and walked and talked among men and being put to death, came forth from death and walked once more among men.

Now, I am aware that there may be doubts and reservations concerning the reality of the resurrection and the personal immortality of man, but unless this be fact, there would be futility before us. Through His atonement, the Savior made it possible for all of us to return to a glory that we cannot even imagine.

Sad as it is, I know that London's time had come. I know that through Christ we will all be resurrected and through the saving grace of His atonement, all, if we live worthy, will be able to be with her in eternity.

I know that London will be dropping pebbles in the pool of her new home, the one she came from in the first place, among those loved ones that have gone on before.

As much as he misses her, Brook is doing admirably well as a result of a feeling in his heart that a Higher Power had called her home. It was simply meant to be.

London now lies next to the aunt she never knew in life, but in many ways resembles so much, Rochelle. In the same family plot lies Mike and Frances Wilson, who made it possible to purchase Three Bear, as well as Walt and Shirley Butcher, trusted managers of Parade Rest Ranch for so many years. Someday, and I hope not too soon, we intend to rest there along with our loved ones just one mile from our home that we love so much.

TWINKLE 21

Living in Those Twilight Years

Those twilight years are creeping up on us. I will write this Twinkle for both of us and from the perspective of an 84-year old couple. As we forge ahead into the inevitable unknown, which will be a new experience for us, it occurred to me that our life now may be the *inevitable unknown* to many younger people. We used to wonder what it would be like to live at our age. To answer that question, I will share some of the feelings and maybe even the romanticism of two people still in love at our age.

Somewhere between birth and near the end of a long life, we live in what I will refer to as the *twilight years*. Linda's dad, her brother Norman, our daughter Rochelle, and granddaughter London were never able to live in that time of their life. Death at such an early age seems so untimely. Yet we are not in control of such things. I am grateful we are not, for if we were, we would never allow our loved ones to leave us nor would we leave them and thus we would thwart the plan of God. It's been said that, "Everybody wants to go to heaven, but nobody wants to die to get there."

Linda and I are now crossing into that time of our life when we carry a calendar, not for business and social events, but to make and keep our doctor appointments. We are blessed with a lot of time on our hands, or it would be very difficult to keep those appointments.

We have also noticed that, in our younger days, if we had a problem we could go to a doctor and come out feeling better or at least come out with a solution. That does not seem to be the case in our waning (twilight) years. Since our ailments are mostly age related, they often require an appointment with a specialist. That takes about a month, then that specialist refers us to another and that normally takes another month to get that appointment and so on. I guess it is timely because earlier in our life, we just did not have time for all this newfound time-consuming activity.

One seldom knows in advance when the time of our departure is at hand. Some are not afraid of death but worry about the process of getting to that point. Some pass through the door into the next phase easily and perhaps even untimely to those who are left behind. To others the door seems to have rather rusty hinges and does not want to open quite yet.

I quote now from an editorial regarding suffering that was quoted in my Dear Uncle Glen Cameron's funeral.

> Sometimes we have lessons to learn. God has his way of teaching them. Suffering was made a part of mortality. We must taste the bitter to appreciate the sweet. There is strength to be gained from suffering. There is depth of understanding, sympathy for others, even for the Christ who suffered so much for all of us, that we may suffer less. The atonement of Christ was one of suffering, yet there would be no gospel, no salvation without it. Yes, the Lord permits suffering. He has His purposes. Let us trust in His justice and mercy.

It was 64 years ago when I was on a mission in England, and I was talking to a couple of old British blokes. One said to me, "I just want to live while I live, and die when I die and be done with it." Another retorted, "I just want the Lord to keep me alive as long as I live." Two different perspectives, I suppose, one was just enduring life, the other wanted to enjoy life to the end.

We are told in Mathew, ". . . he that shall endure unto the end, the same shall be saved." Will the enduring be a challenge or a blessing, or will it be both? Will we just endure, or will we enjoy the enduring, both physically and spiritually?

On my mission, I was talking to another old English gentleman, a common laborer. In my mind I can still see him. He was dressed in an old suit coat and loose tie as was the tradition. He was all dirty from digging a trench in the street. I got to talking to him and he said, "I'll be glad when I am safely dead, mate!"

Perhaps if we can enjoy the enduring and do what the Lord would have us do while in this life, being "safely dead" may mean as Paul said in Timothy, "I have fought a good fight, I have finished my course, I have kept the faith: Henceforth there is laid up for me a crown of righteousness . . ." I can more fully endorse what my English friend said by changing just one word to, "I'll be glad when I am safely HOME."

Paul also says to *be of good cheer*. This earthly life is only a temporary state and I believe that *in the twinkling of an eye* we will be going back to the home from whence we came. There, the travail of this life will be put behind us and the glory found there, in our earthly vocabulary, will be indescribable.

Our South Fremont High School class of 1957 reunion was held yesterday. We are one of the few classes that are still holding class reunions. Linda's North Fremont reunions have ceased because of attrition. We used to hold them about every 5 years, but since we are getting fewer in number and would rather view than be viewed, we have been having them annually. We don't know who we said good-bye to that may not be with us next year. It has been 72 years since we graduated into the big wide world of opportunity. It is always so good to see those of our formative high school years.

At this last reunion, the first observation was, *there sure are a lot of "old" people here.* (I didn't have a mirror.) The signs of aging were there, but my classmates' spirits were still the same. How blessed Linda and I felt, for, if I counted correctly, out of the 20 present only 5 had spouses still with them. It was interesting as we listened to each tell of their life's journey.

I couldn't help but recall with some familiarity, the following quick overview of how the stages of our lives go.

Does any of this look familiar to you? Linda and I have been blessed to ride on many of these wheels together. I think this comic image will resonate with all who are of our age. Many have also ridden on these wheels during the different "Twinkles" of their lives.

The Wheels of Life

Then my Aunt Eva Cameron sent the following poem to me in 1991. She must have been able to relate to it then, as we do now. I will only quote part.

TO A FRIEND (Author unknown)

"Just a line to say I'm living,
That I'm not among the dead.
Tho' I'm getting more forgetful,
And mixed up in the head.
Sometimes I don't remember
When I stand at the foot of the stair,
If I must go up for something,
Or if I just come down from there."

I think we have all been here, if not literally, in other ways. We are now entering a new chapter, or *twinkle*, of our lives. This is different, however, than any in the past.

It was Mark Batterson who said, "The greatest chapters in history always begin with risk, and the same is true with the chapters of your life."

The risks that lie ahead of us in this twinkle of our lives are yet unknown. We have always been able to a large degree, and with the help from above, be more in control of our future.

However, today is not in our rear-view mirror yet and we can't see into the future with as much clarity as in the past. Physical health and necessities are changing. Consequently, time restraints, commitments, obligations, and priorities are also changing as we continue on this earthly journey.

We are so blessed to be able to look back through all those twinkling years together, not without trials and hardships, but with few regrets. We have raised a family that we are so proud of. We have always enjoyed traveling, normally with our kids in the spring and by ourselves or with family, friends or siblings in the fall. We have taken 28 major trips from Australia to Eastern Europe, from Alaska to South Africa.

We have enjoyed Maui as our special family getaway for 41 years. (We are just hearing about the fires that have now destroyed the historical town of Lahaina that we enjoyed so much all these years. We were just there in April. The place where we stay every year was unharmed.) We have had and still have lifelong friends who have helped us both in and out of the workplace that have made our lives full. We have been successful in business. However, our true measure of success lies in our ability to reflect on the positive impact we've made in people's lives, our community, and, most importantly, within our family.

Like Beulah and Bud, and the Swans of the Railroad Ranch, Linda and I have been blessed with a lifetime of love and devotion to each other.

Symbolical of the love that we share

When kneeling across the altar on our wedding day, and we both said, "Yes," we knew we were signing up to be eternal companions. The traditional marriage vows state something like "to have and to hold, from this day forward, for better, for worse, for richer, for poorer, in sickness and in health . . ." Come what may, we will be here for each other as long as the good Lord allows that to be. We do not know what lies ahead, whether it be sickness or health. Our hope is that we will be kept alive physically, mentally and spiritually as "long as we live." But all are subject to the ailments that eventually cause us to pass on to the next existence.

I think John Quincy Adams described this phase of our lives well. I am paraphrasing a little, but when asked the greeting, like we typically do, *"How are you?"* he responded:

> *"John Quincy Adams is just fine, thank you. But, this old house in which I live is becoming creakedy and old. The walls are about to cave in and I fear I am going to have to move out soon, this old tenement is becoming almost uninhabitable. But John Quincy Adams, himself, is quite well, thank you sir, quite well indeed."*

I hope we can remain as upbeat as John Quincy Adams.

Well maybe it's time to switch gears and talk about happier things. Younger people may wonder what it is like to get older? There are not many 84-year-old people that write about their lives. So this may be a little enlightening and fun.

Unlike Beulah and Bud, Linda and I have been blessed to live out most of our lives together. What a blessing that has been. I have sung her praises in my autobiography and have tried to focus this book on the kind of person she is. Linda has always said to her kids and grandkids, "It is not what's on the outside that matters, but what's on the inside that really counts." That probably comes from Mark 7:20, "It is not what is on the outside but what is on the inside that will defile you."

And now let me share my feelings, from my perspective, a little about this person I have been blessed to be with for over 60 years. In Pebble 8, I shared about our marriage from a 50-year perspective. Now 10 years later, our love has still not dimmed. She continues to be the "wind beneath my wings."

Now, this may seem a little personal and out of character for those who know us, but I will tell you anyway. This is Sunday morning and Linda and I were dressed to go to church. I came from my office and Linda came from the bedroom and we intersected in the kitchen. She held out her arms and with that twinkle in her eye looked up into mine and said "kiss me" and I obliged.

As we embraced, more like squeezed each other, an unusual thing happened. From the phone in my shirt pocket, Frank Sinatra started to sing. Since we were already tightly embraced, I took her hand in mine and we started to dance cheek to cheek. That was something we used to like to do, the old-fashioned way. I guess Pandora must have been up on my phone and by her squeezing tightly against my chest, we pushed the play button. So, we danced away in the kitchen. We danced, even with a little flare as she kept stepping on her oxygen cord and I kept losing my balance. But, it brought back fun memories of many good times and younger years.

I'm sure no one would believe as we slid into our seats in church, barely on time, that this 84-year old couple had been dancing cheek to cheek just 15 minutes before in their kitchen. Just part of the "enjoying the enduring," I guess.

I tell you this because younger people may be shocked to know that us older folks still do such things and if older folks don't do it, they should try it. It keeps the fire burning.

Many write about "young love" and the excitement that goes with that. Few mention the romantic side of older folks' lives. Consequently, those not of our age may wonder what happens to those "old swans" that are blessed to live long lives together? I will answer that from at least our perspective. While it is no longer "young love," it is love that has deepened over the years, and still maintains romanticism. Though the fire within has decreased in intensity, the eternal flame continues.

I believe younger people will be pleasantly surprised to know and look forward to this time in their lives.

We used to sleep really close together, with our goodnight kiss right before we fell asleep. But now, we have to have that kiss before we put on our CPAP masks for the night, which are hooked to machines on opposite sides of the bed.

During the 14 years that I was branch president, I interviewed and counseled many couples before I married them. (Five of which eventually were sealed in the temple.) I would ask them, "Do you love each other?" Of course, they would say "yes."

I would then say something like, "That's great, but, you haven't seen anything yet. Not compared to what it will be. I thought I was in love when we got married, but that was just the beginning of our love as it continued to grow." I also wanted to make sure theirs was more than just *puppy love* that is felt by the young and then fades away as disagreements occur. I've heard that, "Puppy love can lead to a dog's life" and does not last."

That Sunday morning tight squeeze reminded me of another moment, also in the kitchen and on a Sunday afternoon. I related this in Pebble 9. Here is part of it again:

> I had been gone all day to meetings in Ashton, had been fasting and came home bushed. Linda was standing in the kitchen. I didn't say anything, just went over to her and gave her a big hug. As I squeezed her tightly, I could feel her strength come into my body. Finally I started to let go and she kept holding on and said, "Wait a minute, I'm not through with you yet." Soon, our three little boys arrived at the scene and aimed to separate our hug. They pushed between our legs and said,
>
> "Break it up. Break it up."
>
> I chased them all up to our bed, threw them on it, and began to wrestle them. They were all laughing

and I was saying, "I'll teach you guys to try and break
us up."

Linda has never lost the twinkle in her eye. It's almost a
mischievous look.

A few weeks ago, I just returned from town when Linda took me
in my office and sat me down, at first, making me think I was in some
kind of trouble. Instead, the purpose of this little office sit down was
to tell me that she had been reading my book again. She was very
complimentary on how it was written, not just stated facts but me
writing it with feeling. She pulled her chair close to mine and looked
deep into my eyes, with that twinkle in hers, and told me how much
she loved me and kissed me. Of course, I tried to brush it aside, but
this reinforced, again, how much she cares for people and tells them
often how much she thinks about them.

There have been a number of times in our lives when I could have
really been discouraged. We have gone through four fires, the first
one being on the day I signed the papers to buy Three Bear. There
have been times when I tackled a task that seemed insurmountable,
when just brute force wasn't enough, and Linda's encouragement was
needed to push me through to the finish line and succeed.

There was also a time when I was recovering from an operation,
and several problems compounded my recovery that caused me to
become very discouraged. We know that discouragement is one of the
adversary's greatest tools. For a few months, I felt like I had lost a light
and I felt hollow inside. I had never felt that way before and wondered
how I could get through it all. Linda, of course, knew what was going
on and sat me down, as she had before. as I mentioned earlier. She
told me that she had faith in me and that we had gone through tough
times before and that I could do it.

In the meantime, I read several times about Job and the trials
that he went through where he lost everything including his sons and
daughters, and his body became covered with boils. His wife finally
said to him, "Curse God and die." Now I don't pretend to equate
my troubles to Job's, but his wife's admonition was to "curse God

and die," whereas my wife's message was, "You can do it." With that encouragement, and help from on High, I did.

While writing this, I was listening to Josh Groban sing, "You Raise Me Up." It seemed applicable to us. I will refer to just one verse.

> *You raise me up, so I can stand on mountains.*
> *You raise me up, to walk on stormy seas.*
> *I am strong, when I am on your shoulders.*
> *You raise me up to more than I can be.*

It would have been really ironic if, when dancing in the kitchen, Frank would have been singing his song entitled, "Linda," it goes:

> *When I go to sleep, I never count sheep,*
> *I count all the charms about Linda*

Now it doesn't seem unusual to me for songs to be written about Linda.

In checking further, I found that there are more songs written about "Linda" than any other name. There are 79 songs written about Linda and 17 about Linda Lu.

So I thought I would check and see how many songs are written about Clyde. What a let down, I could only find one. It goes like this.

> *Let me tell you 'bout Ahab The Arab . . .*
> *every evening about midnight,*
> *He'd jump on his camel named Clyde.*

I knew I had married up, but when I married Linda, I had no idea how much.

Then I found a poem which didn't make it into a song but I was hoping would elevate my status. But it was still a downer.

> *Here lies Clyde, who wouldn't be neat*
> *He entered this house without wiping his feet.*

Ironically, a few days ago, I was talking with a TV tech guy in Dallas, Texas, and, of course, he asked my name. I told him, "Clyde."

He said, "Oh, that reminds me of a 1978 Clint Eastwood movie, *Every Which Way But Loose* and the phrase, 'Right turn, Clyde,'" and he chuckled when he said it.

Now I had real hope. Maybe this would help level the playing field with Linda. I looked up the movie on YouTube and watched some clips. It showed a number of different scenarios, such as when a policeman came to the stopped car, and Clint's character would say, "Right turn, Clyde." Clyde, sitting in the right passenger seat, would shove his arm out the window as though he were hand signaling for a right-hand turn. However, he did it with such force that the policeman, or other such unsuspecting ne'er-do-wells, would get knocked out or at least fall to the ground. Then Clint's character and Clyde would just drive away.

My hopes were shattered again, especially when I saw that Clyde was a red, long-haired orangutan. These creatures can stand 5' tall, have an arm span of 8 feet, and are 7 times stronger than a human.

But, "hope springs eternal," according to Alexander Pope. Even though my new namesake, "Clyde the orangutan," did not help my self image, I felt that the playing field had been totally leveled. I felt completely vindicated, as far as Linda was concerned. For, you see, when I look in the mirror, I believe I am better looking than the movie's Clyde with his hairy body and big teeth, and I know that Linda would rather kiss me than those thick, protruding lips.

Living in an assisted living senior center is probably the last stop along The Wheels of Life journey, as shown earlier. It is interesting, that through a strange turn of events, we are now residing in such a place. Perhaps we can offer a few insightful observations regarding our assisted living experience. First let me explain how we arrived here.

I have been suffering from a bad lower back for years, and the doctor recommended putting in a pain pump. This would be day surgery, but the after-effects would limit me from bending, stretching and lifting no more than 10 lbs. for 4-6 weeks. Since I was already exceeding those restrictions by taking care of Linda's needs, we decided to go to an assisted living center for a maximum of 4 weeks while I recovered.

It is ironic how these events have unfolded while I have been writing the last twinkle in this book, "Living in the Twilight Years." Assisted living is just what the name implies, and is giving us the opportunity to share *real time*, which is one of the last phases of "enjoying the enduring." This is a beautiful place with people at your beck and call to take care of your every need. Restaurant-style dining, theater, library, fitness room, transportation, and laundry are just a few of the amenities.

Various church services are held which have buoyed us up spiritually for another week. Last Sunday, the sacramental prayers were given in deep soft tones and the ordinance was passed reverently. The only sound difference was, instead of the quiet being broken by a crying child or two, there was a chorus of audible puffs, originated from Linda's portable oxygen and many others all around the room. When the prayers finished, instead of 16-18-year-old boys, those who blessed the sacrament got up with their canes and slowly walked to their seats. Those who passed the sacrament were a little more agile and caneless.

Also, inside the room we met, there was also a parking lot. Instead of cars, there were walkers with wheels on the front and tennis balls on the back, push carts with seats and many parked electric carts that people climbed on after our meeting and then sped off down the hall.

We hope that we will be back home in a month, remembering how grateful we are for people and places like this who are caring and loving to others in the *twilight of their lives*.

There is one last poem that I would like to end with. I suppose I have read and pondered upon it hundreds of times since I first read it over 60 years ago. It has been a help to me and part of my internal guidance system. It is entitled "A Bag of Tools."

Each is given a bag of tools,
A shapeless mass,
A book of rules:
And each must make–
Ere life is flown–
A stumbling Block
Or a stepping stone.

Linda and I have had many stumbling blocks in our lives. We've had to come to terms with the death of our daughter and granddaughter, four major fires, and other catastrophes that caused us to stumble. Those stumbling blocks have turned out to be blessings, as we tried to turn them into stepping stones. For others, we hope we have been able to leave more stepping stones and a little boost, rather than stumbling blocks.

We have now been married for 60+ years. Linda has been the mainstay of my life. She has been the mother of our five children and my love. She has been my encouragement, my confidant, and the rudder that holds my boat steady. She is the litmus test that helps me decide whether I should embark on some wild endeavor. When it comes to social events and visiting in casual situations, I am the one that is in her shadow. Like my dad, I am not very comfortable in social situations. But like her mother, Linda is always outgoing and friendly. It was said of Robert Kennedy that he was not good at small talk, and I can relate to that. I am often more comfortable when she is with me in public. She visits with people openly and freely. It is easy for her to find things to talk about, and she always has nice things to say that lift them.

In writing this book, I have tried to express my love and appreciation for this person that has become "one" with me. I can truthfully say that Linda has been my best friend. She has been a quiet but compelling force and support in my life. I have always known she has my back in whatever I have tried to accomplish in my life. She truly is "the wind beneath my wings."

And lastly I would like to pay homage to my God, my family, my country, and our little community which we love so much, West Yellowstone, Montana.

The days, months and years have passed so quickly since I first came to work here in 1958 as a laundry boy at Three Bear Lodge, and Linda came a year later to work in the Tally Ho Motel. As the biographer, writing about my wife of 60+ years, with her dropping many pebbles in my pond, our life together seems as though it all happened *In the Twinkling of an Eye.*

The End

www.ingramcontent.com/pod-product-compliance
Lightning Source LLC
Chambersburg PA
CBHW060914120626
46553CB00001B/327